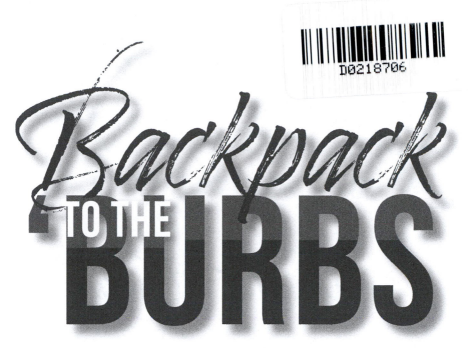

Backpack TO THE BURBS

One Man's Epic Journey
From The Pit To The Palace

BY

STACY J. DODD

Published by Dodd Publishing - Stacy J. Dodd
All Rights Reserved
ISBN 978-1-7363368-0-9
Copyright ©2020 Dodd Publishing
Cover Artwork by Tricia Toomey

Dedication

This book has been a labor of love and reflection for me. I wish to dedicate it to the following: my precious wife, Stephanie, and our kids Dustin and Katie Staggs; my wonderful mom & stepdad, Betty and Al Witt; my amazing dad, James H. Dodd; Rod and Teresa Weber; Harry and Donna Weber; and Debbie Simmons.

Prologue:

I remember like it was yesterday when it was just me and my backpack against the Universe. I would not come out into the open until dark. I did my best to stay hidden on trails and paths through the woods and backroads. I would not look at the passing cars as they sped by me. I was ashamed and humiliated. Towards the end, I could barely speak.

As I walked through church parking lots, I would stop and stare at the signs and the doors and think to myself that they would not want me in there. But there was a longing in my soul that was so deep. There were nights that the stars were so vibrant at times, and my curiosity was incredibly intense. How did I even end up here? I knew there had to be more to me and this life, and I was going to find it.

One

In the beginning, God created man and woman and placed them in the garden. He told them they could have everything beautiful that He made from that day forward. The one thing they couldn't do was touch the forbidden tree. The same goes for us. We must choose one; the two will never co-exist.

I didn't start out as a homeless addict. Every addict is someone's child, and I was no different.

Born in Carthage, Missouri, in 1967, I had terrific parents who were loving, hard-working, and great providers. My mom was a registered nurse anesthetist, and my dad was a very successful car dealer. Their families were also from Missouri and Arkansas. My dad grew up in Bolivar, Missouri, just outside of Springfield, on a dairy farm, and never missed a day of school. My grandfather told him that if he ever missed a day of school, he would have to work on the farm all day. I guess that was a good enough incentive not to skip. My mom was from Marshall, Arkansas. Her father, my grandpa Joe, was a railroad worker. He was getting ready to head to war when the train brought news that the war had ended. I always knew when grandpa was on his way home because his '57 Chevy would smoke like crazy when he drove it up the hill.

My grandpa Joe was a devout Christian. My grandma, Mettie,

loved using a switch and wasn't afraid to use it on anyone who would come into her yard. My grandparents introduced me to the Billy Graham Crusades as they played nightly on the old black and white set in their Harrison, Arkansas home. I loved to visit them and regularly did when my mom put me on a Continental Trailways bus at age eight to travel alone across Arkansas. I spent a lot of time at my grandparent's house.

As I said, my father was a hard-working man, very loving, and a great provider. Everyone loved and admired him. People would come up to me and say, "Oh, you're Jim Dodd's son? He's a fine man!" He always smelled of Old Spice cologne, wore the finest clothes, and drove brand new cars.

Some weekends, my dad would come to get me from my grandparent's house and take me to Silver Dollar City and Dogpatch USA. I bet I visited those amusement parks at least 20 times during my young life. What he didn't realize that I knew was that he stashed a bottle of liquor under the bed at the hotel. I was too young to understand the dangers of alcohol, but I knew my dad liked to drink.

Usually, about two or three days out of the week, he would call my mom to see if she needed anything from the store. We knew that if he didn't show up within 30 minutes, it would be hours before he got home, and there would be a long night of fighting, yelling, and chaos ahead. One of my earliest memories is of my parents fighting. My brother would take me into his bedroom and play to distract me from the yelling and screaming. One evening during one of their many fights, my father broke my mother's arm. I remember riding in the long Cadillac over the snowy and icy roads to the babysitter's house while mom went to the doctor. Then one night, she loaded my older brother and me into the car with our bags packed, and the three of us left my dad, never to return.

My mom took us to Paris, Texas, where we stayed for about a year. While there, I gave her a pretty good scare. One day, she came home and couldn't find me. She frantically searched everywhere. She found me in my closet, standing on a chair with a rope around my neck. When she asked me why I would do that, I told her that I had seen it in an old western movie. I could have died, but by God's grace, she found me in time.

We moved again—this time to a small town outside of Little Rock, Arkansas, called Benton. I remember vividly one day in Benton standing on a ladder outside, looking up at the clouds and reaching for them. I could feel God's presence, and I knew something was there; I just didn't know what it was. I've never forgotten that day, and I've always wondered what it all meant.

Our next stop was a town called Dermott. It was a small town of about 4,000 people in southeast Arkansas surrounded by cotton fields and just a few miles from the Mississippi River banks. My mom moved to a small town to keep my brother and me out of trouble and provide a safe environment for us. In Dermott, there were railroad tracks that ran through the middle of the town. Those tracks separated the black community from the white community, and I was told never to go across the tracks alone. I was never told why, but I knew I would be in deep trouble if I got caught.

My mom's best friend was the wife of an Arkansas state senator. She knew everyone in town and made it her business to know their business. She would drive around at night, snooping on people, and did her best to find the latest "news." She had maids that cleaned her house, cooked for her, and did whatever other chores needed to be done. As the wife of a senator, she was very involved in local elections. I remember riding with her and my mom through the cotton fields until we would arrive at the small shacks in the middle of the fields. I would get out of the car and deliver absentee ballots to the family inside.

My mom was a registered nurse anesthetist and worked on call 24 hours a day, seven days a week, at two hospitals. She would be gone for sometimes 12 hours at a time doing surgeries. That left me at the house alone with my older brother. My brother was eight years older than me and had a group of friends who would often come by our house to talk, laugh, and have fun. One night, as we were joking around, my brother and his friends said, "Try a puff of this cigarette."

Wanting to fit in, I tried it and started coughing, trying to catch my breath. Everyone in the room started laughing. It began as just something funny that didn't mean to cause any harm. But it wasn't long until I had my own pack of cigarettes.

It also wasn't too long until I took a drink of a beer one night when my mom and one of her friends were having a cookout.

Not too long after this, I tried marijuana for the first time.

And it was not too long after that that I began to seek cigarettes and marijuana regularly.

It felt good to be hanging out with the 'older' kids. They would go to certain areas of the county and shoot guns, fish, go to racetracks, and do all kinds of crazy things. My brother was a bookworm type and really didn't want to go with them. I would beg my mom repeatedly until she would allow me to go with them.

I remember the first time I got very drunk. We all went to Lake Chicot, where I learned to ski that day. I also drank 18 Miller Ponies and became so drunk that I got sick while I was in the boat. The guy who owned the boat was livid that I had thrown up and dumped gas on me. It burned a giant spot on my stomach. Later, the guys snuck me home that night under the radar.

In the evenings, the older guys would get in four-wheel-drive pickups and fly across the railroad tracks and drive to the African American neighborhoods. They'd throw eggs and water balloons at the families who were minding their own business. They drove past them, yelling, screaming, and laughing. It wasn't until much later in life that I realized the horrible things that I witnessed at such an early age. I always wondered down deep in my heart why they were so mean to these people that had done nothing to them. I don't think I've ever found an answer to those questions. But what I had witnessed those nights made me love the African American people even more. I knew they had done nothing to deserve the treatment they were receiving.

One day, I was riding bikes with my best friend from school. We were in the 3rd grade at the time. After spending the afternoon with him, it was time for my friend to go home. I wanted to ride with him, but he lived on the outskirts of town, and I knew that my mom had set boundaries for me as to how far out of town I could ride. I figured that I could ride with him just a little way and get home before anyone knew it. So, I broke the rules as always and went farther than I was supposed to go. After going about a mile past the boundary that my mom had set, I said goodbye, and I turned around and headed back towards home.

Within about three minutes, I heard tires screeching. There was an interstate right past the railroad tracks that my friend was crossing. I didn't make much of it and just kept riding fast to get home. The next thing I know, my mom burst through the door at our home, grabbed me, and started screaming at me. She told me that my friend had gotten run over by a car and was dead.

She told me that the police thought I was with him and that they were currently searching the ditches alongside the interstate for my body. I got the whipping of my life for breaking the rules that day. I know my mom was scared, but I realized that she loved me enough to punish me because she was trying to teach me to obey her.

Because mom worked such long hours, she would always leave money on the table every morning; this was her way of caring for me and being a good mother. What she didn't know was not only did she leave enough for me to buy what I needed, but there was also some left to buy cigarettes and marijuana. And because she worked such long hours, it allowed me to do more things I knew I was not supposed to do.

I would ride my bicycle all over town, including across the tracks where I wasn't supposed to go. One of those places was a local pool hall called the Big D. I would stand on chairs, play foosball, and shoot pool at the age of seven. One day at the Big D, I heard a commotion outside around the side of a big truck. I peeked around the corner and saw two men rolling on the ground fighting with giant knives trying to kill each other. It was a harrowing experience. I was in my 40's when I realized the trauma caused by what I witnessed that day.

I had a very close friend named David. He was the meanest kid in town. We would ride our bikes everywhere and stop and talk to everybody. We were involved in everything that was going on in that town. I'll never forget when my friend and I were caught by the police shooting our shotguns and 22 rifles in the neighborhood around our house. The officers brought me home to my mom and told her that they trusted her to handle it. She assured them that she would, and she did. You see, my mom was very good with a belt and a switch, and she didn't hesitate to use them at any time. Her mom had taught her well. Sometimes she would whip me so hard I wouldn't be able to go to school the next day.

Nonetheless, I deserved it. You see, I knew right from wrong at a very young age. At the age of seven, I was peeping around the corner to see if anyone were coming so I wouldn't get caught smoking cigarettes. But I never blamed my parents for anything in my life because they did their best to teach me right from wrong. I simply chose to do wrong at times. For example, I used my BB gun to shoot out the church's windows directly across the street from my house. Then, I kissed the preacher's daughter out back in the shed when no one was around. No, I was just very precocious and enjoyed the thrill of not getting caught, like when a friend and I were smoking in a small shed behind a neighbor's house. About 30 minutes later, we heard fire engines and discovered we'd accidentally burned down the barn. We hurried home, not saying a word to anyone.

I tried to do the right thing at times. I even went to church sometimes. I had two friends that were much older and lived two blocks down the street. Their dad was extremely strict, and he used to beat them badly. One evening they invited me to go to a revival at their church. The preacher showed a video of some kids riding a motorcycle, and they rode off the side of a cliff. The accident caused one boy to be decapitated. The video then cut to Satan standing there laughing while holding a pitchfork with fire and brimstone burning in the background. Of course, I was scared to death, and I ran down the aisle to 'get saved.' The problem was that I had no idea what that meant, nor did I know who Jesus was or what the gospel was. It was just a scare tactic, and being eight years old, I fell for it. When I got home, my mom was furious.

One of my best friends had a family that owned a 2,000-acre cotton farm. I went out to his house one weekend and fell in love with the country life. They had farmhands that lived down the street in a house that was on blocks. These farmhands were extremely poor and had nine kids. And all nine kids had kids. My mom allowed me to go out to his country home on this farm every single weekend for years.

Since my dad wasn't active in my life, this family adopted me and taught me how to hunt, fish, and farm, among other things. The weekends were so much fun; we would coon hunt at night, wading through swamps that were full of snakes and mosquitoes. Wherever the dogs went, we went. I could shoot and kill two doves flying simultaneously with a 20-gauge pump shotgun at the age of 8. We would farm during the day, and if it were raining, we would run trotlines and fish on the Mississippi River from daylight till dark.

Whatever hunting season it was, that's what we did. If it was squirrel season, we hunted squirrels. When it was rabbit season, we hunted rabbits. The family that owned the farm had a deer camp along the Mississippi River, where they would also invite me to join them during deer season. There was also a place just outside of town called the "7 Devil's Bottom." It was a place known for excellent hog hunting. It was also well-known because many folks who went in never came out. I went in a few times without my mom knowing. I could feel the evil in the atmosphere. I quickly became terrified and ran out as fast as I could.

On many sweltering summer days, we would walk the bayous killing snakes that were hanging in the trees just for something to do. We would also carry irrigation pipes and lay watermelons underneath the fresh, cold water to eat at lunchtime. The farmers would drop us off with the hoe, a water jug, and watermelon and leave us in the cotton fields chopping Johnson grass. When they paid us, we spent our money at the skating rink on Saturday nights. We earned eight dollars a day for a whole day's work. These farmers were well off. They would take us to the lake where we would ski, fish, and, of course, drink. And with drinking, would come fighting.

Sometimes, the drunken fistfights would last well into the night. I would hide in one of the rooms so that I wouldn't get involved. But oh, how I loved being there and being a part of that family. They were like a substitute for what I was missing. I had an incredibly close bond with the dad. There were times that we would ride along the levee of the Mississippi River in his Twin I-Beam Ford pickup. We'd talk, laugh, and weave back and forth on the levee while drinking whiskey until he would get so drunk that I would have to drive. I was scared to death and could barely see over the steering wheel, but we always made it home.

I learned so much for a young boy during those summers. Working in the cotton fields, I learned how to chop cotton, pick cotton, stomp cotton – you name it, I did it. We would also dig tunnels in the cotton trailers. That would set us up for more mischief at night. One evening while hanging out between the farmhouses, we decided to throw eggs at passing cars while hiding in one of the cotton trailers. We aimed and managed to hit a passing

4-wheel drive truck. What we didn't expect was the man to slam on his brakes and back up. In the pitch-black night, he got out of his truck and hollered, "You have just 60-seconds before I start shooting!" We didn't wait around long as his first shot ricocheted off the side of the trailer. My friends and I scrambled over the back walls and took off running as fast as we could. We heard four more shots go into the trailer as we disappeared into the darkness of the cotton fields.

After summer ended, it was time for school to begin again. My mom put me in a private school outside of town with about 300 students. I learned later that racism played a big part in that decision. The name of the school was Bellaire Academy. The mascot was an Indian Warrior, complete with arrowhead logos on the football helmets and jerseys. Later, I would see how this would tie in with my Spirit-led journey and archeological treasure hunts that I will discuss in later chapters.

I would ride to school each day with an older kid who drove a Ford Cobra. That car was a beast! The school was only three miles outside of town, but he went at 100 MPH, passing vehicles on bridges and always knocking at death's door. As a passenger, I was so scared and wondered how I managed to arrive without a scratch. This was another miracle of God's hand of protection over me.

At school, I was very involved in basketball. My friend and I were in the fourth grade but were placed on the sixth-grade basketball team. It was so 'cool' to be on the older team. When

I got my first pair of Converse shoes, I felt like I was in the big leagues. I was invincible, I thought. But, when I first stepped on that court, I was so nervous. Those nerves soon went away, and I ended up loving every second of it.

Hanging out unsupervised with older kids was a rush, but it also came with an evil that I learned the hard way. Until now, I have never spoken of it to anyone because of the trauma it caused me. One night, my friend and I were in an old shed behind the neighbor's house, smoking pot and drinking. One of the older guys from the neighborhood showed up and started laughing and joking with us. Then he casually stated that it would be funny if we would perform oral sex on him. We ran out of the building quickly and never mentioned much of it after that.

Today when I look back, it makes me angry. I carried that around with me for decades never spoke about it. I was ashamed, even though nothing happened. I was scared to talk about it because I wasn't sure how people would receive it. Now, as an older man, I look back, and I wonder how many other people he had done that to and what damage this man has done to others, and it still makes me very angry. I wanted to confront him so many times, but I wasn't exactly sure how. When I see him now on social media, he is married and seems to be having a good time. I just want to ask him, "Why did you do that? Do you even remember doing it?" Once again, God protected me without me ever knowing He was there.

Two

"Before I shaped you in the womb, I knew all about you. Before you saw the light of day, I had holy plans for you: A prophet to the nations — that's what I had in mind for you." Jeremiah 1:5 MSG

One day, out of the blue, my mom called me into the living room and told me we were moving again. I was devastated. Moving was difficult for me since I had spent from the first to the sixth grade in Dermott, and I didn't want to leave my friends whom I loved deeply. Still, the summer after my sixth-grade year, we headed to West Monroe, Louisiana.

West Monroe was the biggest city I'd ever lived in, and as hard as it was to leave Dermott, it was exciting moving to a new environment. But the excitement turned to fear as I saw the size of the new school I'd be attending. Would I fit in with the crowd? Would I make friends? All these questions ran through my mind. I became frustrated and wondered why we had to move so often and why we always had to 'start over.' This time, there would be no private school. The school in West Monroe consisted of half black and half white students, and there was lots of adversity and tension there. Still, I managed to seek out new friends who smoked and drank like me. We moved to a newly built, large apartment community. On the weekends, my friends and I would go from apartment to apartment to party. We would go everywhere within that apartment complex, smoking and drinking and just having fun. As always, the friends I had were older than me. My drinking and drug use were my way of coping with my emotions and fitting in wherever I ended up.

Again, after a brief stay in West Monroe, the dreaded announcement came that we were moving to Tulsa. I resented having to move again. I began to resent my mom. I still loved her, but I questioned why we had to go. Nevertheless, I left my friends, my school, and my routine and headed north. Once we got to Tulsa, the cycle began again for me. I was in the 8th grade when I started Nimitz Jr. High School, which was the largest school I'd ever attended. Again, I sought out older kids who smoked and drank as I did. I had the coolest BMX Mongoose bike and rode it to meet up with my new friends at the local movie theater to watch the midnight shows on the weekends. We'd drink beer, smoke, and ride our bikes to the river and on the trails. I didn't have a care in the world.

During this time, my mom had met a very friendly dentist. She administered anesthesia to his patients while she worked at a local hospital. They struck up a friendship that turned into a romantic relationship. I was so happy to see my mother happy. After being alone for ten years, she deserved it. There had been many nights that she would weep in her room when she thought no one could hear, but I did hear.

As their relationship strengthened, so did my relationship with a rough group of guys, and soon, my marijuana habit escalated. They introduced me to a man who worked at a local convenience store that had a steady supply. I began staying at this man's apartment on the weekends. Eventually, I convinced my mom to allow me to live with him and his wife. My friends and I would sneak into the golf courses at night and smoke weed. Before long, I was staying out all night with no accountability.

My mom married the dentist in 1981, and he became my stepdad. They moved to Saudi Arabia to do some work. However, it wasn't long after she left that she began getting reports that I was skipping school and heading down a dangerous path. She eventually hired a private detective to follow me and discovered my new and very destructive lifestyle. My mom grew weary of my rebellion and deemed me uncontrollable. She got in touch with my real dad and decided that I would live with him for good.

My dad had also remarried and had a lovely family. I had been riding a Greyhound bus from Tulsa to Joplin regularly to visit my dad. One weekend when I arrived at my dad's home, I got the news once again. I was heartbroken, though, when my dad told me that I would not return to Tulsa. It seemed like I had just started to fit in with new friends and everything I loved. Uprooted again, I moved in with my dad and my new stepfamily.

My dad and his family lived in Joplin, Missouri, in a beautiful home at Shoal Creek. Their home was on the outskirts of town, and everyone loved coming to the Grand Falls to swim. It was the place to go for teenagers who liked to party. My new school,

Parkwood High, was huge and intimidating, but I had learned to seek out the kids who were like me by this time. On the first day, I learned that the school did not offer a class that I wanted to take. So, I had to be placed in a study hall or ISS (in-school suspension) during that period. This was also the place that the kids who'd been suspended had to go. I had found an open door for me to spot the ones who smoked weed, drank, and partied hard. I was quickly introduced to my weed supplier and fell right back into my 'routine.'

During the summer, my dad would take my stepbrother and me to a place close by called Redings Mill Pool. This pool was the size of a football field and was spring-fed weekly from the Shoal Creek, so the water was always cold. Everyone spent their summers there. My dad wouldn't stay with us. He would drop us off at 11 a.m. and pick us up at 6 p.m. every day. My new friends would arrive, and we would leave the pool and head to the nearby Redings Mill Bridge to smoke weed and drink. The water at the bridge was even colder than at the pool. After a few hours there, we'd wade out waist deep and throw rocks at the giant wasp's nests under the bridge. When the nests would fall, the wasps started to attack. We would dive underwater to escape their wrath until the nests floated downstream, taking the swarm with it. Some people would say we were crazy, but to us, this was living the life!

Summer nights in Joplin were just as packed as the days. On the weekends, we would camp out in the woods, sometimes the whole weekend. Friday and Saturday nights, we go skating at Keely's

Silver Wheels skating rink. During the second service, we'd sneak out with our girlfriends to the woods to smoke pot and drink.

I didn't just party all the time. I was expected to work around the house, and my dad paid me for my chores. He believed in working hard and doing your best at any job you were given. I mowed the yard, cleaned the gutters, and kept the garage clean. If I missed a spot, he would show me. He wouldn't pay me until it was done right. He was such a patient teacher and had a great work ethic. That is what made him such a successful businessman.

When I got older, my dad took the money that my grandparents had left me and bought me a car. He was so proud to be able to purchase this car for me. It was a 1976 Ford Elite. The car was huge and wasn't considered cool, but there was no way that I was going to hurt his feelings by telling him. On the upside, I was finally mobile! With mobility came my first outside job working as a dishwasher at a local restaurant. Even though I was still smoking weed and drinking, I never let that interfere with my job. I worked hard and made sure my job came first. In my off time, I would go on float trips and camping trips with my friends. I stayed high and drunk until it was time to go back to work.

It was during this time that I met the girl of my dreams. She was the most beautiful woman I'd ever seen, and I found myself wanting to be with her 24-hours a day. We would camp at Elk Creek, attend heavy metal concerts, and go to keg parties. I was so serious about her and wanted to marry her. I had also begun to experiment with shooting up drugs and using cocaine. It was an exhilarating rush like I'd never experienced, and I wanted more. As my drug use increased, I began to deteriorate. I was oblivious to what was happening. I thought that if I had money to buy marijuana steadily, I'd be okay. My mom had moved to Saudi Arabia for a short time, but she returned to the states every year for a visit. One summer during vacation, I traveled to Washington, DC, to meet up with her and spend some time catching up. When I returned to Joplin, I discovered that my girlfriend had left me for one of my friends. I was beyond devastated. This 'friend' had been one that had told me to dump her because she was so horrible. What a great 'friend,' huh? The pain that I felt was unbearable. I felt ugly, lonely like no one would ever love me again. I needed to forget her, but how?

Another close friend of mine told me that he could help me. He was a confidant and someone I loved deeply as a friend, almost like a brother. He began to take me to heavy metal bars featuring beautiful girls in Spandex. I drank excessively and snorted cocaine to try to forget the pain, but nothing helped. My heart had been ripped to shreds, and I felt that there was no hope. I continued to frequent the bars and bury myself in alcohol and drugs as a substitute. I went to party after party to fit in with the group, trying to find validation.

It wasn't long before I had my first DUI and went to jail. Then another DUI, then more jail. With my third DUI, my ignition was locked and had a breathalyzer attached to it so that my car wouldn't start unless I breathed into it and passed. Each time I went to jail, my dad bailed me out. I began to not worry about the consequences of my actions. Afterward, I realized that getting bailed out was not always the best thing. Soon, I was introduced to methamphetamines. It was cheaper, and the high lasted much longer. It was the best feeling I'd ever felt. I felt like Superman. I could stay up and not eat for days and weeks at a time. In the beginning, I was so productive. I got so much done and seemed to feel better than ever. But that was all a delusion.

Eventually, I received my fourth DUI. I was determined to stop drinking. I knew something needed to change. The day after I stopped drinking, I got a letter in the mail informing me that my license had been suspended for ten years. I was angry. I thought to myself, "Here I am, trying to do the right thing, and now this?"

My parents never pushed church or religion on me. I went a few times to Sunday School and Vacation Bible School as a kid, but nothing more. While living in Arkansas, my mom got milked out of some money by the local Church of Christ. She was so hurt that she never went back. I'm not even sure she ever stepped foot inside another church. Still, in all, I always felt that small whisper at times that God was real. Little did I know that my path would show me how real He is.

One afternoon as I was walking up the road, I began to look at the beautiful trees lining the street. It was a lovely spring day, and the sun felt good shining down on my face. The breeze was gentle. In that breeze, I felt God speaking to me in my spirit.

He said, "Son, you can have everything beautiful in this world, or you can have your addiction. But you can't have both. If you continue to drink, you'll end up walking everywhere you go for the rest of your life."

From that moment on, I never took another drink of alcohol.

But all my money and resources instead went to my meth addiction.

Three

"For I know the plans I have for you, "declares the Lord, "plans to prosper you and not to harm you, plans to give you hope and a future. Then you will call on me and come and pray to me, and I will listen to you. You will seek me and find me when you seek me with all of your heart." Jeremiah 29:11-13 NIV

Having a suspended license didn't stop me. My dad ended up giving me another vehicle. It was a 1984 Ford F150 pickup, way cooler than the 1976 "behemoth" I had earlier. I remember his words saying, "Son, this is the last thing I'll be able to buy you. Please take good care of it." I assured him that I would, and off I went to buy more drugs.

One day, I was driving the streets, and I passed by a dumpster filled with all kinds of things like merchandise and furniture. As I stopped, I thought that I could make a living taking things that no one wanted anymore and trade them for money. I could still feed my habit and not have to work for another person. I saw it as saving the earth by saving things from being smashed into the planet. It was a way not to be accountable to anyone and not function like the rest of society. It wasn't too long before I traveled the alleyways of Joplin looking for things I could sell and trade for drugs. My friends and I called it pillaging. Yes, we ended up dumpster diving, but it was never for food. It was always to find things of value to trade for more drugs. I became extremely good at this new lifestyle.

All my keg party friends ended up running meth labs. All my concert-going friends had meth labs. I had friends in Oklahoma, Missouri, Arkansas, and Kansas that ran meth labs, and I would travel from place to place to get my fix. I stayed high for months at a time. I didn't have any contact with my family except to get money. At any point, I could have died, and no one would have known where I was.

Across that four-state area, my friends also grew marijuana on sacred Indian burial grounds. They knew that the feds wouldn't look there since it was protected tribal property. We took five-gallon buckets, scissors, and baggies out into the woods at night and processed the weed. We'd then bury the full buckets in locations across those states so that we could dig them up when we needed more weed or money. We lived off the land by hunting and fishing for our food. I was able to stay high and make money. During this time, my mom would send me money, too, usually $100 at a time. I would always give her some sob story to make her feel bad. She had no idea that sending me money was enabling me to keep a steady supply of drugs.

One of my friends had a wealthy dad. We convinced him to buy an old restaurant to remodel and open the first heavy metal bar in Joplin. While it was being renovated, I worked at his Army Surplus store to make a little money. After the bar was built, my friend and I worked there. I started as the janitor and ended up as the General Manager. My first weekend, we hosted a "Battle of the Bands" at the bar. It was a huge success, and we made $10,000.00 in cash. I had friends coming from a four-state area to the bar every weekend to party. My drug use became so bad that my family in Joplin wanted to send me to Memphis to live with my mom. I was reluctant to leave, but I decided that maybe Memphis would give me a new start. I packed up my Firebird, my new girlfriend, and a quarter-pound of weed and took off to Memphis.

While driving to Memphis, my girlfriend and I talked about starting over. Maybe we could do the right thing and get the help we needed to kick the drugs. My mom and stepdad were so welcoming, and they pledged to help us in any way they could. I enrolled in State Tech College, intent on getting my accounting degree. In Memphis, I noticed that the cops were not around as much. Heck, I could walk down the street, smoking weed and drinking a beer, and no one batted an eye.

My parents were so excited that I was on the right track. It was evident that I was making a positive change, or so they thought. Then, the inevitable day came when I ran out of marijuana. I had to find a supplier, but I didn't know anyone in Memphis. I searched out different parts of Memphis and ended up in Midtown at a place called Printer's Alley. It was easy for me to make new friends there, and soon I got the hook up for a steady supply.

One day, I was told the weed shipment would be delayed for one week. A guy that I had met mentioned that he could get me a rock. Now, I had done cocaine but had never smoked crack cocaine. I had heard that once you do, you can't stop, and the addiction to crack was so strong that it took over your willpower immediately. I was reluctant to try it, but I took my first hit one night at the bar.

For the next two years, I experienced the worst addiction a human being could ever imagine. It made me forget about my family, my hopes, my dreams, everything. All I could think of was how to get enough money to get that next fix. My girlfriend started running around and disappeared into a dark world made up of my worst nightmares. Mom wanted me out of her house, so she found a sixth-floor apartment for me close to the hospital where she worked. She ended up paying the rent on it. I would walk to the local Burger King and panhandle for money in the drive-thru. Since my mom worked across the street at the hospital, I would call her begging for money. She would give me $20 each day, and I would walk straight to a crack house at Dixie Homes to buy crack. Dixie Homes was not a safe place for anyone to go, especially a skinny white guy. But it never scared me. I was in the middle of my addiction, fearless, and crazy. I didn't care about anything but getting more crack.

One night, I was in my apartment on the sixth floor, hanging out of the window wanting to die. I cried out to God. I cried and cried. My addiction was so bad that I had pawned my car to a drug dealer and then would sneak back to his hotel at four in the morning to steal it back. I sold all my belongings, including my furniture, to have money to buy crack. Meth addiction is nothing compared to the devastation of crack cocaine. I thought I was going to die. Obtaining crack daily in a vicious place like Memphis was not for the weak. I was sprayed with mace point-blank while in a dangerous neighborhood by some drug dealers who tried to rob me. They have many tactics to get what they want and don't care what they must do to get it. Their biggest scheme was to entice young girls into the drug world by getting them hooked on crack, then use them up and destroy their lives. They would pay young kids on bikes to deliver the drugs because the dealers knew the cops wouldn't mess with the kids. Many of the dealers didn't even use drugs. They just kept it going to fund their lavish lifestyle. Human lives meant nothing to these people.

My mom pleaded with me over and over to stop. Eventually, she had no choice but to contact my dad, and they decided that the best thing would be for me to go back to Joplin on the next plane.

When I arrived back in Joplin, not much had changed. I was in one of the worse shapes of my life, physically, mentally, and spiritually. My dad had told me that I would have a place to lay my head as long as he was alive. Looking back, I can only imagine my father's heartbreak seeing my condition and not knowing how he could help me. It didn't take me long to hook up with my old crowd and old habits. Before I knew it, I traveled the four states from meth lab to meth lab to satisfy my addiction.

Believe it or not, I was happy, happy to be addicted to meth, and not crack anymore. With no job, I knew that I needed to begin pillaging again to fund my habit. I also was involved in some other illegal activity to make a buck. At that time, I didn't care what I had to do because, in my mind, everything was just fine. I took whatever the meth cooks would give me. I had built great relationships with all the dealers and cooks; they trusted me. I interacted with tons of junkies: lawyers, bikers, musicians, business owners, and even bankers. Bail bondsmen were even getting in on the action by promising girls a supply of drugs and freedom for sex. They would bail out the drug dealers and get drugs in return. Imagine my surprise when I discovered that the folks that were supposed to be on the right side of the law were not. It was all a sick, twisted game.

When you are living the drug lifestyle, you quickly discover that not everyone can be trusted. I got ripped off many times during my addiction. While I was waiting in a garage one day to confront a man who had ripped me off, another man showed up. The same thing had happened to him involving the same guy I had been seeking. We became fast friends, and I ended up going to his house many times on old Route 66. His house was located on the outskirts of town, so I felt safe there. I loved his property and was strangely drawn to it. I would find things that he needed in town and have an excuse just to go there and hangout. This property would end up leading me to a grand adventure that is still unfolding before my eyes today.

We started pillaging together and making lots of great

memories. We survived by pillaging and selling discarded things found in the alleys and streets of Joplin. We weren't stealing by any means, as we took what no one else wanted. We had a blast.

The one thing that Missouri has plenty of is rocks. I used to hunt for arrowheads with my friends and find something discarded, thinking it was an arrowhead, only to be told that it was 'just a rock.' I was determined to find artifacts, so their brush off was frustrating to me. They would always tell me that my finds were not authentic. One day while at my friend's property, I happened to look down at the rocks embedded in the ground. I noticed that they had unusual patterns with different colors and shapes. These rocks were wedged so tightly that a truck could run over them, and they wouldn't budge. Every time I visited the property, I took ample notice of these incredible rocks. I started a collection, but I hid them from my friends. They always said, "Dodd's trippin' on rocks!" We would all laugh, but it didn't stop me.

The property was located close to a spring, and I would use that water to wash off the rocks. I noticed that when I washed them off, their patterns became clearer. Sometimes, I would stand outside, acting as a lookout for the guys inside. As I arranged the rocks in a circle, I took a hose and watered the rocks while smoking a joint. It sounds funny, I know, but I discovered something incredible. My eyes were opened to see birds in trees, buffalos, snakes on the ground, and even images of people embedded in the rocks! I knew that these rocks were unique, but I felt in my soul that God intended for me to discover the secret treasure in these rocks.

These patterns were symbolic, and I knew that this was the find of a lifetime for me, and I wanted to discover more.

My obsession with these rocks was almost as great as my addiction to drugs. I felt a strange connection to the property. I didn't want to leave, so my friend told me I could sleep in the barn. One night, while in the barn, I had a vivid dream. It was right after I had discovered the rocks. I dreamed that I was standing outside the barn, and there were thousands of baby white wolves around me. They began licking my fingers as the mother wolf stood by approvingly. I was sure that this dream had something to do with the rock findings, but I never really understood its significance.

Each day, I would discover new rocks and new patterns within the stones. It was fascinating to see. Each rock seemed to tell a story or recreate a scene. Soon, I had piles of rocks in different areas of the property. The more I found, the more I dug. It was indeed a mystery that I was determined to solve. I would put some in my backpack to show the people in my life. I loved sharing my treasure with people.

I learned that it was not safe to go to the city of Joplin after 10 p.m., not because of the crime, but because the cops would patrol and stop anyone they saw. One night, my friends begged me to go with them. I was adamant that I would not go because I knew that the cops would get us. They kept on and on until I gave in. I grabbed my backpack, and we piled in the small pick-up truck. Of course, it had no tags.

Within 15 minutes of our journey, the police passed us on the road. We turned in the first driveway we saw and jumped out of the truck. I threw my backpack into the woods, and we started running. The cops turned around and began to chase us down. They chased us from midnight to daylight through the woods, past the old Route 66 Drive-In, and into Joplin. The police had the entire force looking for us, including the dogs. By the time they caught us, we were ripped to shreds. Looking back, it was like God was chasing us. We tried our best to get away from Him, choosing a life of destruction and waste. But He wanted to use us for His glory to minister to others. I thank God that He was relentless in His pursuit.

Things didn't change after that. I would still ride my bike everywhere, pillage for stuff to sell so I could stay high. At one point, I was coming down off my meth high after weeks of no sleep and no food. I fell asleep in the back of a trailer. The top half of my body was folded over in the trailer, but my body's bottom half was on the ground. The next thing I know, bounty hunters were pointing machine guns at my head and screaming, "Wake up, boy!" I was so out of it that I shouted back, "Get out of my yard!" Looking back on it now, that was insane!

Other times, I would ride my bike for miles on country roads after midnight to go from one meth lab to another. One night as I was riding, a wolf exited the woods and ran alongside me for a while. It never acted viciously. It just ran with me as I rode. It was strange because I wasn't scared. I recalled my dream of the wolves and wondered if it was all related to the archeological discovery I had made. Though the rock discovery kept me busy, it didn't put a dent in my drug use. One thing that comes from drug abuse is malnutrition. The malnutrition from the drugs deteriorated my body so much that it began to affect my bones, especially my feet. There were times that I could barely walk. But the addiction was greater than the pain.

One thing never changed, and that was the love of my parents towards me. I never doubted their love, but they each showed it differently. I was humiliated, dirty, and gross, yet my father would always look for me and find me. He would always tell me he loved me, and he knew I would be okay. He repeatedly told me that he needed to talk to me about something important. Still, at the age of 33, I was too busy being homeless, jobless, and self-destructive to care about anyone but myself. I never would take the time to see him. My mom and stepdad were still living in Memphis during this time. My mom's love was manifested by providing me money for my needs. When I was little, she left money on the table for me, and later she would send me $100 bills through the post office. I would sneak through trails from the woods to the post office on North Main Street in Joplin. The lady at the post office would have my small white envelope behind the counter. She saved it for me as I had no address. I'm curious as to what she thought in her mind when I showed up. I would love to meet her one day and ask. Mom had no idea that she was enabling me during that time, but she eventually learned that I needed tough love.

One night, she and my stepdad decided to find an Al-Anon

group for me in Memphis. On the way there, they got lost and ended up at another support group meeting. That group stopped their meeting so that Mom could pour out her heart to them about my situation. The next morning, she called me and said, "Stacy, I can't help you anymore. Until you clean up your life, don't call me. Until you change your life, don't ask me for any more money." She also told me that a lady named Arlene that she worked with had her entire church in Orange Mound praying for me. She said that they were "sicking God on me." True to her word, the money stopped coming.

I began living in the woods near the Ozark Christian College and abandoned houses all over the county. I never ventured out during the day. I had many reasons. The shame of being homeless in my hometown was overwhelming. I had warrants out for my arrest. I would use the railroad tracks, trails in the woods, and secret pathways to go everywhere. I could go from meth lab to meth lab without ever getting on a public street or sidewalk. I learned to master the darkness. I learned how to have thousands of dollars in methamphetamines in my pocket without having a job. I learned how to steal expensive items and rationalize it by saying that I kept the world going around. I would never steal from a working man, though. That was the insanity of my addiction.

I knew the time of the police's shift changes, and I knew when and where they patrolled. I knew exactly what I could get away with and continued to push the boundaries. I knew that if I had everything set up, I could do whatever I wanted between 4:15

a.m. and 5:15 a.m. The city was open to me during that time. I even stole an expensive piece of equipment and rode it through the middle of town. There I was, 120 lbs., my long hair flowing, smoking a joint and whistling "Dixie" with a smile on my face.

I wasn't scared of anything; I wasn't afraid of the woods. Copperheads and rattlesnakes didn't scare me. Being in places where I could get killed by drug dealers didn't scare me. I wasn't scared because I had no conscience - I had nothing - I had no God. But there were times that I would stare up at the stars at night and wonder if there was supposed to be more to my life. I would often cry when I was alone. I was so ashamed of what my life had become. Even my friends no longer welcomed me in their house. If I needed a place to sleep, I would sleep in the barn. I was filthy. I had become a liar, junkie, and a thief: the three things that I said I would never become. These things were now my life and almost my death.

I remember vividly sitting on a log in the woods by the Ozark Christian College. I was filled with overwhelming guilt and deep sadness. I was exhausted, filthy dirty, and weeping uncontrollably, cried out, "God, if you are real, I need you. I need you NOW! I don't want to live anymore! My life is over, and if you're real, please help me. I need you!"

I was at the end of myself.

Right where I needed to be.

Right where God wanted me to be.

Four

John replied in the words of Isaiah the prophet, "I am the voice of one calling in the wilderness, 'Make straight the way for the Lord.'"
John 1:23 NIV

I had been arrested so often, doing 30-, 60- and 90-day stints in the county jail for meth possession and other drug-related charges. One night while in jail, I was crying so hard that I seriously thought I had a stroke. I was empty. I walked in circles in my pod, spiritually and emotionally exhausted and mentally numb. My memory was gone. This lasted for an entire day. However, the next morning was different. I woke up refreshed and renewed. Maybe I had an intense spiritual awakening, who knows? All I know is that I felt different, and it felt good. My hopes and dreams were coming back to me. I felt that God had caused this miraculous awakening in my soul.

I was awaiting rehab when a guard came and told me I had a visitor. It was my stepbrother. He looked at me with tears in his eyes and told me my father had passed away. It was cancer. That is what he had wanted to talk to me about those months ago, but I was too busy to make time to visit him, to take the time to spend time with him during his last dying days on earth. I begged to go to the funeral, but my family would not bail me out. It was only about $100, but they were trying to teach me a lesson. Even the guards were furious at the way I was being treated. I laid in my cell for days crying. I was escorted to my father's funeral, wearing an orange jumpsuit and shackled like a murderer. I was so ashamed. I had lost my best friend, my cheerleader, who loved me unconditionally. I could only spend 10 minutes with him at the funeral before I had to be taken back to jail. He was gone forever, and he never knew how much I loved him.

Alone in my cell, I felt that my soul had been ripped from the depths of my body. It was the worst emotional pain of my life so far. Not only was I a liar, junkie, and thief, but I was a failure as a son and a brother. I was ready to get clean. I was told that a bed would open in the rehab facility soon, and I was prepared to make a change. After spending an additional 40 days in jail, the bed never became available in rehab. They had no choice but to put me out on the street again, with nowhere to go and not a penny to my name.

My dad had always told me that I would always have a place to call home and lay my head as long as he was alive. I walked six miles to my father's home, intending to make it right. I wanted to apologize for the horrible things I had done and everything I had put my family through. Still, they wouldn't even answer the door. My stepmother refused to let me in. I was not welcomed there any longer.

I became a walking zombie. I had no one, no home, nothing.

Eventually, I went to the only place I knew: the drug dealers and the meth cooks. I knew that I could make some money and survive by using and selling drugs. While waiting for my upcoming court date, I was taken in by a man who felt sorry for me. He let me stay in his shop east of town. It had no running water or electricity, so I had to take five-gallon buckets across the street to fill with water to take a bath. Some of my friends would come and stay with me frequently. The shop outside looked like an abandoned building, but the inside looked like The Ringling Brother's Circus.

Again, I would walk the streets of Joplin at night so humiliated. I wouldn't even look at the passing cars for fear that someone would recognize me. I didn't want my lifelong friends to see me in my current condition. My addiction had taken its toll on me and ruined my mind, body, and soul. As I walked through church parking lots, I would stop and stare at the signs and the doors and think to myself that they would not want me in there. I felt there was no hope for someone like me.

On the morning of my court date, I had a hooded sweatshirt, a pair of shorts, and my backpack. I had also stolen two more sets of clothes from the Salvation Army parking lot bin, and they were stuffed in my backpack. My court officer told me that I would probably be given four-year probation on the condition that I would leave the state of Missouri and not return. I had reached out to my mom, who had provided me a bus ticket to Memphis. Before my court hearing, I stood in the parking lot and shot up meth. I stood in front of the judge, pled guilty, ticket in my backpack, ready to get on the bus to Memphis when he handed down the sentence of six years in prison.

Wait! That's not how this was supposed to go! Shocked, I fell to my knees and was transported to jail. I wanted to die. They put me in a padded cell, and I woke up with the court paper in my hand. My release date was set for 2007. I had been on meth for ten years. I couldn't make it for 24-hours, much less six years.

I'll never forget the ride to the state prison. I was in a van with 12 other men, most of whom I knew. My hands and feet were shackled to bars bolted to the floor. When we drove through the prison gates, I recalled all of the stories my mom and dad told me about prison. My worst nightmares were about to come true, and I couldn't stop it.

I would have given anything not to have been checked into the prison that day. The repeated offers of my mom offering me a full ride to college played through my mind. My parents had begged me to make better choices, but I ignored them. I chose to live my own life on my terms. Now, I was entering a place filled with the worst of the worst, and I was one of them. The check-in process was horrible. I had no idea what to expect. I had only seen prison through the tv shows, and this was nothing like Hollywood.

I had to be placed in a padded cell on arrival. I was suicidal. In my heart, I knew my life was over. Once I was taken off suicide watch, I had to be housed in the diagnostics facility. Everyone from first-time offenders to hardened murderers was there. We went through processing and were classified. No cigarettes were allowed. It was very close quarters, and there were many fights. I spent three months in the diagnostic facility before I was moved to the next house. I shared that house with ten other inmates who were African American males. I thought to myself, "I'm in trouble now." At night, they would stay up playing cards, and by the morning, they would be fighting each other over the game. That was their life and their way of coping with being removed from society. Over time, these men turned out to be great friends and some of the nicest men I'd ever met.

I was assigned a job in the cafeteria to make breakfast for over 2,000 inmates. I would get up every morning at 2:30 a.m. and be at work by 4 a.m. to stir oatmeal with a boat paddle. There was a man assigned to train me, and we would talk about different things. One morning, I told him that I had been reading my Bible. He looked at me and said, "Boy, I bet you don't even know the names of God."

He was right; I didn't. But from that moment on, I was determined to learn all I could. Every day following my shift, I headed back to my cell, showered, and grabbed my Bible to read. I began to recall all the times I spent in the local jail and realized there had always been a Bible within reach. I didn't know much about the Bible. I only knew a few stories about the Ark, the whale, Moses, David, and Goliath: the stuff you learn in Vacation Bible School. I knew a few religious symbols, but I didn't know anything deeper. I didn't have a clue about who Jesus was, or the Gospel, or how it related to me. I had read in Genesis about the

Creation, which was exciting. But after about the second or third chapter, nothing made sense, so I put it down. I thought the whole Bible was like that. Now that I had six years to do nothing, I had plenty of time to spare, so I started reading my Bible from front to back. I ended up in the New Testament reading about this cat named Jesus. I had no idea there were stories like this in the Bible. The more I read, the more exciting the stories became. It was like a spiritual adventure of a lifetime. But I had no one to teach me what it all meant. So, I would read, lay my Bible on my chest, and meditate on it. At one point, as I read the Bible in my cell, I came across something that said you must forgive to be forgiven. I had no idea where to begin, and I had no one to teach me how to forgive. I truly hated some people, so I asked God to teach me how to forgive.

Desperate to learn more, I signed up for the Catholic and Protestant church services. I was seeking God harder than ever. When I looked around at my life, I knew I needed to change. My way wasn't working. No one visited me; no one called me. I had no one to call because no one wanted to hear their phone ring and hear me on the other end. My past was terrible, and the only remarkable accomplishment I had was graduating high school. I wanted God in my life. I wanted to feel Him and know Him. I wanted to live for Him and not for me.

A man would come to speak to us each week at the prison. I came to admire this man. I wondered why he would take time on his day off to visit me, a criminal, the lowest of the low. That same man led me to Christ, and I was baptized in front of hundreds of other inmates. I always thought to myself, if I can ever change my life, I want to do what this man does. I want to speak to inmates as this man does. I can't think of a more worthy cause than to talk to people at rock-bottom and help them discover how God can change their lives.

"...yet now I am happy, not because you were made sorry, but because your sorrow led you to repentance. For you became sorrowful as God intended and so were not harmed in any way by us."   2 Corinthians 7:9 NIV

Five

Time passes more slowly when you are alone, and I was so alone. I had no visits for 14 months. Most of the inmates had weekly visitors, but not me. My mom wrote to me and sent me money occasionally. My dad had died, and my stepfamily did not want to hear from me. During this time, God was teaching me so much, things I could never learn anywhere else. I thought back on when I had entered the prison. I was placed in isolation because I was suicidal. As I sat in that padded cell, a prison guard slid a book with no cover through the door slot. It was a book titled "Battlefield of the Mind" by Joyce Meyer. This book transformed my mind. It helped me to understand the battle raging within me.

My addiction was so overwhelming that I had to be caged like an animal so that I physically could not get drugs. I had been so smart and creative, always manipulating my way to get drugs and whatever else I wanted to stay ahead of the game. I had not been completely clean since the age of seven. Still, here I was in a maximum-security prison with my Bible in my hand, talking to God. God adopted me and made me His own. He was teaching me that I didn't need anyone or any material thing. I needed to rely only on Him. I needed His Holy Spirit to work in me.

I sincerely believe that He wants to teach everyone that same truth when it is the right time for them. For me, it was when I was rock-bottom at the age of 33. Little did I know what was happening inside my heart, mind, and soul inside those prison walls. I know now that the 'gift' of rock-bottom creates something inside a human that cannot be bought, sold, or earned. It is a gift from above created from pain, hurt, and injustice. It makes an unconditional love that man has for his fellow human beings. It causes a man to come into a prison to speak to other men about the unconditional love of Christ. It treats all men equally. It doesn't matter who they are or what they've done. It is what I call the gift of rock-bottom, and it's the gift of salvation that causes those who accept it to be able to love other human beings without judgment.

I learned of a program available in prison that was a 180 Day Cognitive Behavioral Therapy Program. It was an original therapeutic community. I went to my case manager and begged to be accepted into the program. I let him know that everything I'd ever done wrong was to get more drugs. He told me that he didn't think I'd get accepted because I didn't qualify. Most inmates had to serve five years before they qualified for the program. One night, about four weeks later, the guards came in at almost 2 a.m. yelling, "Dodd, pack your bags! You're going to treatment!" I packed as quickly as I could and got ready to go.

This program was not a cakewalk. There were over 300 rules designed to break you down and stress you out. First, they shave your head and make you tuck in your shirt. You must march for

180 days. You can't even lean back on your bunk between the hours of 6 a.m. and 10:30 p.m. There are no holidays – not even Christmas or your birthday. My job in this program was to lead a group of men every morning and encourage them not to give up. This was a tremendous challenge considering there were 200 inmates who were not happy at all. It was in this program that God first introduced the words Turning Point. The actual name of the program was Bridges to Freedom and Turning Point. Later, God would use the words "Turning Point" in my ministry to show His sovereignty and intentionality.

I was able to complete this strict program, and it changed my life completely. I learned that my actions hurt people, not just myself, but mainly my family. I learned about accountability. If one person broke a rule in this program, they punished us all. For instance, if you talked in the chow hall while eating, you just cost 200 people their cigarette break. At that moment, they all wanted to kill you.

As hard as that program was, I was incredibly happy. I was comfortable in prison. I was walking around for the first time in my life totally free, whistling "Dixie." I didn't want to leave. I never actually told anyone that, but I did not want to leave prison. I didn't know if I would be able to stay clean. I didn't know how I would make a living and provide for myself. After I graduated from the program, I had to go back into the general population. They would release me from prison early, but I had to have a reliable place to stay. This was called a home plan. My mom decided to give me one last chance. I believe that a parent's love for their child is the closest thing we will ever experience next to God's love for us on this earth in our lifetime. She and my stepdad went to the parole office daily, fighting to get me back home. It took four months to complete my interstate compact. I remember the day I was sitting in the waiting room, getting ready to leave prison for the final time. I reflected on the time spent there and the people that I had encountered along the way. The prison had the best counselors I had ever experienced in my life. They taught us how to begin again. I have never come across more emphatic teaching than that since then. As I was leaving, one of my counselors came to me and told me what a great job I had done. He told me that I should consider helping others one day. I never forgot his face, and I never forgot his simple words of encouragement to me. I never saw him again, but his words kept me going when I wanted to quit.

When I received my belongings that I had arrived with, I had one backpack. Inside were the two changes of clothes that I had stolen from the Salvation Army bin in Joplin and two small pendants that I had found in the alleyways of Joplin. I also had one softcover Bible that was given to me by a man in the prison. I believed this man felt sorry for me. I was clean and getting ready to step back into the world for the first time as a terrified man. I had nothing but the contents in that backpack with which to attempt to rebuild my life. But I did have a secret inside that I had no idea was going to take over. I was ready for my new journey.

As I walked out of those prison gates, I crossed that boundary line between prison and freedom. I spoke out loud and clear, "I am never going back in there."

My mom sent me $20 to help get me home to Memphis. I rode on a Greyhound bus from St. Joseph, MO, all the way to Memphis, TN. It was kind of funny because that bus ran right through Joplin, MO, in the middle of the night. I passed the streets and alleys that I traveled throughout my lifetime. Those alleys were the same ones I wandered around in looking for something to trade for drugs. Those streets were the same ones I used to go to high school that held many great memories. Those streets were also the same ones that I had traveled when I had been homeless, humiliated, ashamed, and hungry. Now I was on a Greyhound bus passing through with no chemicals in my body. God had a plan for me. He had taken over my life and started me on a new journey with Him in the lead.

When the bus pulled into Memphis, I was scared like a small child on the inside. I was being given another chance, one that I didn't deserve. I was so scared that I wouldn't be able to stay clean. There were so many 'what ifs' going through my head. What if I failed again? What if I relapsed? If I did, I would go straight back to prison. What if no one gave me a chance because of my past? I was scared. Yes, I arrived in Memphis with nothing but a backpack, but I was drug-free and had accepted Christ this time. Over the past two decades, I learned that it's not the size of your backpack that counts, but rather what's inside. I had my Bible in mine. This was my guidebook for my new life.

Stepping off the bus, my stepfather, Al, greeted me. He didn't recognize me because I had gained 40 lbs. My head was shaved. He took me to a small apartment where my mom greeted me with open arms. I was ashamed of how I had treated my mom and stepdad during the darkest times of my addiction. I knew my mom loved me, but I knew that she probably didn't think I could change this time. I had failed so many times in the past, been in 30-day treatments multiple times. My mom had paid for acupuncture and expensive programs. The only thing that had made the difference was tough love.

Oh, how her heart broke for me when she found out I was going to prison. Her voice screaming and weeping on the phone was a sound I will never forget. I imagine that down deep inside, she must have felt that some of this was her fault. She didn't stick it out with my dad when he was in the middle of his alcoholism. She moved to Saudi Arabia when I was in the eighth grade, leaving me here. I'm sure she had many thoughts of 'if only.' We all have those thoughts at times, hindsight being 20/20 and all. Maybe she could have made a decision that would have never ended with me going to prison. Regardless of what she thought, I decided to do the things I did. I never blamed my parents for my situation because I knew right from wrong. I knew it from a very early age and felt it when my mom took a switch or a belt to my backside. Reflecting on my life, I knew then that what I did was wrong at the age of six or seven. I would sneak around. I was seven years old when I was smoking a cigarette behind a giant oak tree, peeking around to make sure no one was coming. If you're sneaking, then there is an excellent chance you are doing something wrong. Have no secrets. This will give you peace.

I stayed in a tiny bedroom on a daybed at their small Midtown Memphis apartment. My mom had not told my brother that I was in prison, as she was embarrassed. She didn't want him to know. I told him that I was coming to Memphis for a new start once again and looking for a job. He suggested that I go to the unemployment office. A few days later, I stood in a long line until I finally was able to see a man in the office. He filled out a form, shook his head, and said, "I'm not sure they'll give you a chance, but I'm going to send you down to a national electronics manufacturer, and we'll see what happens. They may give you a shot. Good luck, young man!"

Since I was on parole, I had to report to the parole office in downtown Memphis every two weeks until further notice. I had no idea what to expect. I waited in another long line until I finally met my parole officer. He was a big man with a badge that he wore around his neck. He had just returned from revoking the parole on local gang members. I told him that I didn't think anyone would hire me, and he looked at me and said, "Dodd, somebody can give you a chance." I had to present a check stub to him every month, or my parole would be revoked, and I would go back to prison. I was scared to death and felt very alone. I didn't have a resume or anything positive to add, but I knew deep in my heart that I was kind and I loved people. For the first time in my life, I was attempting to be a productive citizen. This time, there were no chemicals involved: no marijuana, no alcohol.

I know that God never tempts us, but He does test us. Two of these tests came early in my recovery. One day I was walking my dog in the apartment complex. I looked down and saw a small bag of weed on the ground. I picked it up and smelled it. It was the good stuff. I threw it into a bush. I felt like huge eyes were looking down on me. There was a deep humming sound as well. I went back to the apartment and began to think. Usually, I would have stashed that for use at a later time. I would have never thrown out good weed. Never! I went back outside and fetched it out of the bush. I proceeded to the dumpster and threw it in. My thoughts were, what if a young kid found it?

The next test came as I was shopping at a garage sale with my girlfriend. I looked down on the ground and saw a $100 bill. The skills I had developed in life had taught me a few things. I casually moved over and put my foot on it. I made sure no one was looking, and I reached down to scratch my ankle and grabbed the bill. As I looked around, I saw a very hardworking Hispanic lady that oversaw the sale. Once again, I felt those giant eyes and heard the humming noise. I walked over to the lady and handed her the money. Another lady tried to claim it was hers, but we both believed she was lying.

For the first time in my life, I listened to God thoroughly. I did the right thing, not once, but twice. I started to rebuild my severely damaged integrity. Within two weeks of these events, God began to pour His blessings out on me. I had passed the small tests and was moving into His plan. He was watching; I did not doubt in my mind. The following morning, I went to that company for an interview. I got the job! I was a temporary employee and made $8/hour with no benefits. I worked about 60-70 hours per week, but I didn't mind the long hours. I was so happy to have that job and that chance. I showed up for work early and stayed late.

What I didn't realize is that it was only a temporary job. After 90 days, they let all the temporary employees go and hired new ones to avoid paying benefits, giving raises, and other things that employees deserved. A corporate leader came in one day and stood on a big platform told us our jobs would be permanent if we worked hard, came in on time, and did everything we were supposed to do. Not long after that, we were called into the office one by one and given pink slips.

I had worked so hard in the department I was in, and it didn't go unnoticed. My manager pulled me aside one day and told me to see him before I left if anything ever happened to my position there. He knew what was about to happen, but he couldn't tell me. When I received my pink slip, my heart was shattered. I was so afraid I wouldn't have the pay stubs to give to my parole officer. I remembered what my manager had said, so I found him before I left. He told me that he had a friend who owned a business, and he would like to send me there for an interview. I immediately reached out to that man and was hired. After a bit, I was promoted to foreman, then advanced to a supervisor, then the lead supervisor on the first shift. I stayed at that company for 11 years.

I was learning new things all the time – things that I didn't know would be used for promotions later in life. I learned to use a computer, send emails, and communicate with professionals worldwide. I learned to lead a team of people, conduct performance evaluations, and hand out disciplinary actions. I learned how to lead groups of diverse backgrounds. Many of the people on my team were African Americans or Hispanic. I never looked at their color or nationality. I have always loved people and based relationships on character and how we treated each other. I would laugh and joke with my teams because I learned to be open and love them with all my heart.

Then I got some devastating news. In 2006, I was diagnosed with Hepatitis C from my years of drug abuse and alcoholism. Less than a year later, I was diagnosed with bladder cancer. The doctor simply walked into the office, told me I had cancer, and walked out. My mom and stepdad were in the room with me when I got the news. We cried and cried. I thought I was going to die. I questioned God. "I've been clean for over five years and have been living for You. Why do I have cancer?" I didn't understand. Some people would give up and turn their back on God, but my prayer life intensified. My desire to be in a relationship with God grew stronger and stronger each day. That doctor never took the time to explain treatment options or anything else for that matter. I learned through that experience that not all doctors are good doctors. No earthly title determines integrity: no doctor, pastor, or other markers. Only a person's actions tell the story of who they are. I went to another doctor and began months and months of treatments involving hundreds of catheters and even a round of chemotherapy. After three years, the Hepatitis and Cancer were gone.

And I will give you treasures hidden in the darkness— secret riches. I will do this so you may know that I am the Lord, the God of Israel, the one who calls you by name. Isaiah 45:3 NLT

As my time in Memphis went on, my mind couldn't help but recall the property just west of Joplin, where I discovered the incredible rocks. I thought about them often while I was in prison. I would cry a lot. I felt so strongly that God had revealed a precious treasure to me. Now that I was clean, things were becoming more evident. I felt like I had let God down. I knew in my heart that I needed to return to Joplin and investigate with a clear mind and a clear heart. However, I was unable to leave the state of Tennessee for two years. Once that time was up, I flew on a small plane from Memphis to Joplin. I stayed in a hotel, and the next morning I took a taxi to the property. It was sweltering that day – 110 degrees! The driver let me out close to the property. For the past five years, I had worried myself sick that something would happen to this precious discovery. Upon walking up to the area, I saw it.

Everything was exactly where I left it! I was so overwhelmed at the sight of all the rocks. There were so many pieces to study. Time always seemed to stand still on that property. I had witnessed many strange things on that piece of land, some during the day and many at night. There was something so extraordinary there. I recalled how I even ended up at that land on the border of Missouri, Kansas, and Oklahoma. Time was running out, and I knew I had to leave soon, so I gathered five pieces that I thought were significant, placed them in my backpack, and began my return journey to Memphis. I was worried about what the flight attendants would believe as they checked my bags and found the rocks. It's funny as I look back on it, but post 9/11 security didn't play. Nothing was said, and I continued back to Memphis.

When I got home, I went back to my routine of work and my new life. While I was cleaning my apartment, I looked up at one of the rocks on the shelf and noticed something odd. It looked like it was in the shape of an eagle. I started looking at them more intensely, and the more I looked, the more I saw. I studied their patterns and shapes. While I continued to grow in my faith, the blessings continued to flow. For the next ten years, I would return to that unique property to investigate the treasure. I found stones in the shapes of mammoths, eagles, bears, and many apes. At first, I questioned myself and wondered how it could be true. But the more I tried to convince myself I was wrong, and the more God revealed that it was His precious treasure to me. What was I supposed to do with this discovery? Well, I knew I needed to have it authenticated by archeological authorities. Still, I had to show evidence of human artistry in the stone.

I sent a few pieces to some artifact rating authorities in the U.S. I received authentication on some of the hand axes. I created a detailed report and submitted it to the Missouri Archeological Society. Upon viewing the photos, they issued me an official site number, 23 JP 1222. We named the site the Old Route 66 Zoo.

There were so many different shapes of the stones that we thought it was a great fit, and it was located on the old Route 66. Back when I first discovered the rocks, I was still using drugs. My friend and I set up a communication system with walkie-talkies to let him know who was on the property and if they were okay to be there.

One day, I had set up a circle of rocks and was hosing them down. A young man showed up and told me a story about him and his grandfather searching for buried treasure. They would dig 10' deep looking for that treasure, and never finding anything. He said they had never looked on this side of Old Route 66. Of course, his story intrigued me. The legend was that an old outlaw buried a treasure close by, and it was so big that no one man could ever carry it out. There was another story about some old outlaws that robbed trains and were chased by Indians. They buried their treasure, and it was supposed to be in that area, again so big that no man could ever carry it alone. As I continued my research, I always thought about what the man had said to me. Maybe the rocks were the treasure. They indeed were unique. Many had shapes of animals and creatures, but some had an evil motive behind them. There were also depictions of the devil and lots of nasty looking creatures.

Over ten years, I probably made over 20 trips back and forth from Memphis to Joplin. I retrieved the artifacts, cleaned them up, and started a collection. I feel my transformation began with the discovery of these rocks. I believe that God used them to show me a great treasure, took it back, cleaned me up, and transformed me for His Glory, then returned the treasure to me. My obligation with the discovery and the revelation of these rocks is to God alone. My goal is to show this beautiful treasure to the world. It is indeed more precious than any treasure of gold or silver. Why? I'm glad you asked! The longer I kept these stones close to me, the more I learned about them. I discovered that the creatures depicted were from the Pleistocene era and before. The rocks had a secret. They are continuing to reveal their secret little by little even now.

Jesus said to them, "Come with me. I'll make a new kind of fisherman out of you. I'll show you how to catch men and women instead of perch and bass." They didn't ask questions, but simply dropped their nets and followed.   Matthew 4:19-20 MSG

When you start your life over with Jesus Christ at the center, each day is new. The old has passed away, and each day brings new blessings and new revelations. One day I met a beautiful lady. We went out to dinner for our first date, and when I saw her, I knew she was the one that God had planned for me. Other relationships had been based on what I had wanted, and they didn't work. This time, I wanted to have a relationship with the one God designed for me. Not only was she beautiful, but she was also a hard worker and a single mom with a tremendous spirit. She let me know very quickly that she didn't need me, and she and her kids would be fine by themselves. I admired everything about her: her strength and determination, her work ethic, her personality, and her character. Oh, did I mention she was beautiful? We began to attend church together at a church plant at the local YMCA. We'd get there early to set up chairs and help get the building ready for the services every Sunday. This was the first time that I had ever served in a church.

Not too long after, she and I were married and moved to a city outside of Memphis called Southaven, Mississippi. We built a house there and began going to a larger church in Southaven. When we first started going to this church, I noticed all the men in the church were extremely happy. They were volunteering at church, leading others, and more content than any man I'd been around in my entire life. What was I missing? I had surrendered my life to Christ and been baptized, but there was something I was missing. One day I went to one of our pastors and told him about my past. I told him that I felt it was time to pour into others what God had poured into me. That's when he pointed down the street and said, "Stacy, you need to go to Celebrate Recovery. They need all the help they can get down there." Here is a man who also had a past. He was a former Hell's Angel who had been transformed by the love of Christ. He was a man of integrity, hardworking, and one that I greatly admire to this day. He would even ride his Harley up on the church stage sometimes and use it as a sermon tool.

But I didn't feel worthy to serve God in any capacity. I knew that I was a liar, junkie, and a thief. I had no idea how God could use someone as bad as me. I understood how bad I used to be. Not long after the conversation with the pastor, I contacted the man who was leading Celebrate Recovery. He told me that they met on Friday nights. What a letdown! I was so discouraged because I worked the second shift and could not attend the meetings.

But God ...

Less than two weeks later, my boss called me into his office. He slammed some papers down on his desk and said, "Well, he's not going to do his job. You want to come to the first shift and take over his job?" In a flash, God rearranged things to get me where he wanted me to fulfill His divine purpose in my life. You see, that position would have typically never come available within 20 years without divine supernatural intervention. I immediately went back to the Celebrate Recovery leader and told him that I would like to join the group.

One Sunday, during one of the pastor's messages, it hit me. I never had fully understood the meaning of forgiveness. I never understood grace or that what happened on the Cross was for me. It was like my pilot light was on, but it ignited into a giant flame that day. I understood that I was worthy and that God wanted to use me to tell my story to help others learn about Him and His great love for us. From that point on, I served in the church, leading a small group, and understood the contentment of those men who served because I was now one of them. That flame continues to get brighter and hotter, and I'm the flamethrower. Sometimes it hardly sleeps. It is the fire of the Holy Spirit of God that is revealing His secret to me in great detail.

Within a few short weeks of joining CR, I was leading a group. Then my church invited me to attend a conference in California. In July 2010, I woke up and boarded a jumbo jet to attend a Celebrate Recovery Summit at Saddleback Church in California.

It was so surreal to think about how someone would pay my way to participate in a conference, much less fly anywhere. I was amazed and in awe, but this was all a part of God's grand plan to prepare me for the future He had for me. There were 12 of us who attended, and we stayed in a beautiful hotel. The next morning, we headed to the conference. If you have never experienced Saddleback Church in California, you need to be sure to find their website. The campus was the most beautiful thing I'd ever seen. It was filled with baptism tanks, tombs, and rocks with speakers hidden in them. I entered the building, and there were over 2,000 other grateful believers who were in recovery. God overwhelmed me at that moment. Not too long before, I had been in a prison cell, asking God to use my story. And now here I was in a megachurch in California worshipping God and grateful to be alive. One of the first tasks given to us was to go up to a stranger on campus and tell them our story. Wow! It was a beautiful experience. There was beauty everywhere: on campus, at the gift shop, on the grass, in the sky – everywhere I looked, I wondered if it could get any more beautiful. We were able to drive over to Laguna Beach, and the natural beauty of that landscape took my breath away. It wasn't unusual to see Ferraris, Lamborghinis, and Porches zooming down the highway. I was so amazed by the beautiful things I saw. I thanked God continually as He showed me these sites.

I came back to Mississippi a changed man.

Eight

Then he said to them all: "Whoever wants to be my disciple must deny themselves and take up their cross daily and follow me. Luke 9:23 NIV

Our team had witnessed the magnitude of the global Christ-centered ministry of Celebrate Recovery. Celebrate Recovery was not just a place for hurting people. It was also designed to be a leadership factory with Jesus Christ leading the way. Celebrate Recovery is now in over 35,000 churches around the world, and we were just getting started.

Our church was preaching a sermon series on The Prodigal Son. My pastors asked me if I would share my testimony. For the first time in my life, I stood in front of 1,300 people and shared my story. This is what I had prayed for; this is what God had prepared me for from the time that I was born, experiencing a fractured home, my drug use starting at age seven, and the many struggles of growing up. I shared everything. I spoke with God's authority about my drug use, my life as a liar, junkie, and thief, as well as my time in prison when I first encountered His saving grace. I shared what God had done in my life since prison, and since coming to that church. It was an incredible blessing to be able to share my story!

About two weeks later, my pastor asked to see me in his office. Of course, anytime you are asked to come to the office, it is almost like going to the principal's office at school. I immediately thought, "Did I do something wrong?" I kept going over different things: I had been a small group leader for about six months. I started a small group for Celebrate Recovery that was successful. Was there anything I had done or said out of turn?

When I sat down with him, he explained that the church was planning to expand and start a new campus. They needed a Small Groups Director on campus, and I had been chosen for the position. I sat back and looked at him and asked, "Didn't you hear my testimony a few weeks ago? Why would you choose me when others have been leading small groups for many years?" He looked at me and said, "Stacy, I've prayed about it, and you're the one."

It wasn't long after that I was given the keys to the church building and my own office. I met with him regularly, and he coached me in my new role. He was not only a great leader but became a great friend to me. In my opinion, he was one of the best pastors within that church. So here I was. I had the keys to a massive facility filled with electronics valued at over $4 million, as well as the keys to my own office within that enormous church. I also had the keys to a brand-new home that my wife and I had just built. I looked up at the sky, held all the keys up, and told God that I shouldn't have these keys. He spoke to me and reminded me that He owns it all, including the keys to His Kingdom. He told me and confirmed that He alone gave me those keys. Deep within my heart, the gratitude was unexplainable. I began to do more and more within the church.

Leading in the church was something I never thought I'd ever do. However, as time passed, I felt that I was being called to become a pastor within that church, not the lead pastor, but a pastor. I knew that God had placed a special calling on my life and felt that was the obvious next step in my spiritual journey. However, as conversations took place, I was told that I was disqualified because I had been divorced.

After I had been released from prison, I met a young woman. We dated and got married for all the wrong reasons. Soon after we were married, she began to drink heavily and committed adultery with a co-worker of mine. I tried to reconcile with her, but she refused. I ended up filing for divorce. God showed me the truth and let me know that I had made the wrong decision. But she is the one who committed adultery, not me. Why couldn't I still be a pastor?

I went through about a two-year phase of being very disillusioned with the leadership of the church. One pastor even stood up in front of the congregation and said that he was struggling with lust in his life. I questioned why is he even allowed to stand up there in the pulpit if he is still struggling with that addiction? Why is his sin permissible, and my divorce is not? I questioned why God would allow me to have all these promotions but not let me be a pastor. I looked around at all the pastors in the church, and all I could see was piety and judgmental attitudes that I wasn't worthy enough for them. They all had hidden sins, but they still held the title of pastor. Yet my ex-wife committed adultery, and I was the one to suffer the consequences. It is still hard for me to understand. I continually give my bitterness to God. He knows my heart. I said before that no earthly title determines integrity, no doctor, pastor, or other markers. Only a person's actions tell the story of who they are. Since that time, I have had people approach me and ask me to preach their funeral even before they have passed away.

One day I met a lady in the church. She sat and wept during every service. One Sunday morning, I told my wife that I had to reach out to her. I walked around the pew and sat down beside her. I said, "I don't know who you are or what you are struggling with, but you need to be at Celebrate Recovery with us." Of course, she had no idea what Celebrate Recovery was, but she ended up coming. She was so excited because she had found her Forever Family. She revealed that she had a lung disease and had to carry an oxygen tank with her everywhere. Her doctor had told her that she only had eight months to live. She asked me to preach at her funeral. At that time, being new to leadership, I asked my pastor if I could do that, and he affirmed that I could do that. The funeral day came, and I was surprised to see over 300 bikers standing around her casket. God is so intentional. Her sons were in motorcycle gangs, numerous motorcycle gangs. I asked God to speak through me, and when I stood up to speak, I spoke loudly and with authority for the first time. When I finished, a big burly biker came up to me and said, "Son, that was the Gospel."

As I left the cemetery that day, I looked up at God, and He said, "You are right where I want you to be and doing exactly what I want you to do." He affirmed because I was obedient in walking up to her at church that day, I carried out His will by speaking at her funeral to all those people. God will meticulously plan and arrange many things for one specific conversation to take place.

I am now licensed to perform weddings and have performed many. I have baptized over 800 people in a pool where I am currently employed. I have led over 2,000 people to Christ in the DeSoto County Jail and the community. You see, God knows my heart. He saw my heart and gave me His heart to reach people. God is so intentional. The earthly title of pastor may not be mine, but I have been ordained by God and am His disciple. No man can give that to me, and no man can take it from me. They can plot, plan, scheme, lie, and gossip about you, but they can do nothing to stop God's perfect plan. No, there is no title of pastor in front of my name, but God has placed me in His perfect will to have maximum impact for His Kingdom. God is so intentional.

"Delight yourself in the Lord and He will give you the desires of your heart." Psalm 37:4 MEV

Nine

God has proven over and over that this verse is His truth. My grandpa Joe had an old Bible where he kept notes. Once my life was transformed, my mom handed me that Bible. What a priceless treasure that is to me! I always regretted not knowing enough when I was young to tap into him for wisdom. He loved the Lord more than anyone in the entire family. I can't wait to see him again in paradise.

I'm a firm believer that God can open any human heart at any time. When my dad passed away, I was in jail. My family took what they wanted of his possessions, and I was given nothing, not even a pocketknife. I knew deep in my heart that he would have wanted me to have something to remind me of him. When I was released from prison, I went to the cemetery and took a picture of a photo of him from his memorial stone. I had that picture enlarged and framed, and it still sits in my living room today.

About ten years into my life transformation, after promotions and serving the Lord in church, a manilla envelope showed up in my mailbox. Inside was an object wrapped in toilet paper. It was my dad's ring that he had worn since I was born. A few years later, I found out that it was the ring that my mom had bought for my dad. If I had been able to choose just one thing that belonged to my dad, it would have been that ring. Today, I wear it everywhere

I go. It's over 50 years old, pure gold with five giant diamonds in the center.

The spiritual lesson in that is very significant. God can open any human heart at any time through the power of the Holy Spirit. I didn't ask for the ring; it just showed up. The keynote is that if I hadn't changed my life and been doing so well for so long, I would have never had the honor of wearing my dad's prized possession. When I need to hear my dad's voice of encouragement and love, I look at the ring. I even rub it to feel his presence. God reminds me of His constant presence, too. I can't wait to see them both in paradise.

Ten

It is God's privilege to conceal things and the king's privilege to discover them. Proverbs 25:2 NLT

One day, I received a phone call from one of my friends at church. There had recently been some racial unrest in Memphis at a local Kroger involving a group of teens who had viciously attacked customers in the parking lot. He told me that the DeSoto County Board of Supervisors wanted to speak to us regarding this. DeSoto County, Mississippi, is located right across the state line from Memphis, Tennessee, and Shelby County. Sometimes the bad things in Memphis would spill over into DeSoto County, especially in our schools. Our county government wanted to be proactive. I packed up my Celebrate Recovery Bible, my study books, and all my material centered on youth. Celebrate Recovery had a program for teens called The Landing. This program was designed to help teens overcome bullying, cutting, abandonment, isolation, and many other issues our teens face today.

I was amazed again that I was being called on for advice by those in our local government. When I got there, I presented everything to them, and they loved it. The problem was that students couldn't be forced to go to a Bible-based program. They decided to offer it as an elective for kids to attend after school if they chose to go.

Now the task of how to present this to the parents and students was in front of us.

About a year before this meeting, I had sat in a local coffee shop and worked up an event center business plan. I had envisioned a for-profit venture designed to spread the love of Christ in our community. At the end of the Board of Supervisor's meeting, we decided we needed a place to reveal this plan and program to our community. I asked if we had a community center, and the answer was no. My first thought was, "With a county this big, why don't we have a community center?" On my way home, God spoke to me and said that I need to take the for-profit plan and turn it into a non-profit plan. The next week The Hope Community Center, Inc. was birthed. Varina Hopper at the Horn Lake Chamber of Commerce embraced our mission. She saw the vision and invited us to speak at the morning coffee breaks where Horn Lake chamber members and business leaders were present. I'll never forget that day I stood up in front of that room full of businessmen and women and announced that I was The Hope Center founder. Four days later, I was eating breakfast and saw a newspaper. There I was on the front page! That's how God works.

I had a team of people around me, and we began to develop a mission plan. Early on, I thought that I would need land. I met with the city and started looking for places but couldn't find what I wanted. That is because God had another plan, a better plan. I decided to go around to different schools in our community and tell the staff that I wanted to start a community center. I ended up at an Intermediate School and spoke to the lady at the front desk. She said, "You need to speak to Mr. McKinney." Of course, I didn't know who that was, but I was still excited to see him.

I walked into his office and explained my vision. He smiled, and tears began to roll down his cheeks. He said, "I've been waiting on you." From that moment on, Kenneth McKinney, Sr. and I have been partners in The Hope Center's mission as ambassadors in Christ's Kingdom. God put us together for a reason, for His purpose. Since that time, we have hosted over 100 events.

One day a man showed up unannounced at my office and told me that he was looking for ministries like The Hope Center to be the hands and feet for God in the community. Within 48 hours of that meeting, The Hope Center became an official affiliate with the NBA Memphis Grizzlies Mentor program. It was like a dream come true! Only God could orchestrate something like this.

The Hope Center is still going strong today. Our organization has gained the respect of city and county governments, local law enforcement, business leaders, doctors, bankers, and large churches in the area of all races. We even have corporate support from businesses like Walmart and support from the NW Mississippi Association of Realtors and The Community Foundation of Northwest Mississippi. We have volunteers who mentor the youth and have taken up the cause of The Hope Center. Our vision is to have The Hope Center in every neighborhood. All children need a place to go – a place of encouragement, safety, fun, and a place where they can find peace. It doesn't matter the socioeconomic class or race of anyone. Today we operate out of local schools. We are allowed to use their facilities with no rent, no salaries, and no utility bills. Every dime donated to The Hope Center goes directly back into the kids. We usually meet on Saturdays and play basketball, dance, teach, learn, eat, and pray. We celebrate life together as we teach them about bullying and making the right decisions. The most important thing is that they know we are there for them, loving them unconditionally as God does.

Eleven

"You did not choose me, but I chose you and appointed you so that you might go and bear fruit—fruit that will last—and so that whatever you ask in my name the Father will give you."
John 15:16 NIV

In 2009 when my wife and I first built our home in Southaven, my mom and stepdad were still living in Memphis. Their neighborhood was becoming unsafe for them, so we decided to have them move in with us. We always knew we would be caring for my parents, but I didn't realize it would be so soon.

One day, mom became very ill, and we took her to our local hospital emergency room. Within 48 hours, she was diagnosed with Dementia and Parkinson's. It was such a devastating blow. We began to care for her as best we knew how. One day, I came home and realized its impact on my stepdad and my mom. I had to decide my next step.

I told my wife that I felt I needed to resign from my job to care for my mom. She agreed, and I was able to take FMLA for six months. I became her home health nurse during that time. I learned to change adult diapers and feed my mom every bite of food she took. The first month of caring for mom was not easy. Changing adult diapers is not something that you wake up one day knowing how to do; you must learn. There were days that I would go in to feed her and look into her beautiful eyes and see the eyes of Jesus. He made me realize the love that my mom honestly had for me. I felt I needed to give back to her for all the things she had done for me. Her last act of forgiveness was when she opened her doors and arms to me after I got out of prison. I took her to one of my recovery meetings, and she was given my 10-year chip. Even with dementia, her face would light up when I walked into the room. When I would call her by her middle name, Betty Jean, she would reply, "Yes, darlin.'" It didn't matter where I was in the house. The most important thing was when I would ask her, "Mom, do you know Jesus?" She would say, "Yes, I do."

One morning I went into my mom's room. She was lying on her side, and I rolled her over, but she was unresponsive. I tried to resuscitate her, but Jesus took her home and healed her. I will never regret taking care of my mom for those 14 months. I promised her that I would also take care of her husband, my wonderful stepdad, Al. I promised them both that they would never have to go into an elder care facility. They helped me rebuild my life in a time that I had nothing. The joy of caring for the elderly or someone who can't take care of themselves is an incredible opportunity. It is the chance of a lifetime to allow God's love to flow through you into the lives of others.

In November 2020, my stepfather, Al, joined my mom in the arms of Jesus. There are not enough pages or words to describe what this man meant to me. I became his son all those many years ago, and he, like my mom, loved me unconditionally. I can't wait to see him again. Heaven gets sweeter every day.

"The Lord makes firm the steps of the one who delights in Him;"
Psalm 37:23 NIV

Twelve

Not long after my mom had passed away, I knew that I needed to get back into the workforce. My passion was recovery in the Lord. I had applied to be a coach at a local recovery program, but they didn't hire me when I first applied. I reached out again to the owner of the program and was granted an interview.

I was hired as a Recovery Coach making $8/hour. The company name was Turning Point. It just happened to be the same name as the strict program that I had experienced in prison. Coincidence? Nope, because God is intentional.

My goal was just to pat someone on the back and encourage them. I wanted to use my recovery experience to let others know that they can make it. I had been a manager for over a decade, the Director of Life and Ministry for a local megachurch, and the state representative for Celebrate Recovery. In addition to that, I had a decade of successful recovery myself. I was so excited to be given this role as a Recovery Coach, even though it didn't pay much. I was exactly where God wanted me to be.

My first role there was to lead adolescent groups. I would drive the female patients to their homes in a big white van after the program each day. I usually would have 10-13 ladies in the van, and they would always convince me to stop at Shipley's Donuts. They were so funny in the way they related to each other. They were at rock-bottom and were fighting for their lives. We tend to relate to others through our struggles. They loved each other profoundly, and our staff loved them deeply, as well.

In less than three months, I was called into the office and told that our organization would be repurposing a local hotel into a recovery center. Also, there would be a position open for a Director of Operations, and I was strongly encouraged to apply. I went home that evening and talked to my wife. I told her that my chances of getting that position were slim to none, but I was so honored even to have been considered.

About two months later, I was in Murfreesboro, Tennessee, a city right outside of Nashville, at the Celebrate Recovery East Coast Summit. This conference was just like the ones that were held in Los Angeles at Saddleback Church each year. During one of the worship sessions, I walked outside and saw a young man. He was sitting alone, and I walked up and began talking to him. He started to weep and tell me his story. After a long conversation, he accepted Christ in his heart. I was still reveling in the joy of new salvation when my phone rang. The caller ID revealed it was my boss. He said, "You know that job you applied for? You can have it!"

All my hopes and dreams came true in an instant. I would be making more than I ever thought I would and doing precisely what I was designed to do. My past didn't matter. I knew beyond a shadow of a doubt that this was God's plan for my life. Each new day and new milestone is a grand new adventure and gift for me, given to me by the One who loves me most.

Upon taking on that new role, I was trained in every aspect of inpatient and outpatient clinical recovery programs. Trained on compliance standards, I became an instructor in a nationally recognized de-escalation program. This program is designed to help patients during their most challenging moments so they can stay in recovery. This program is called SAMA, Supported Alternatives to Managing Aggression. I am required to fly to San Antonio to recertify every year. I also became a Certified Peer Support Specialist and eventually moved into the role of Supervisor. I was trained in budgeting, staffing, and all executive management duties.

But my favorite part is that I was able to share the testimony of my faith weekly with over 100 people in recovery. I have had the privilege of baptizing over 800 people in the pool at this facility and lead hundreds to Christ. The faith-based portion of the program is an elective, and patients must freely choose to attend.

I was in a prison cell when God revealed Himself to me. He adopted me into His family and made me His own. He protected me, taught me, equipped me, and loved me when I was unlovable. One of my passions and deepest desires was to go into the jail and speak to the inmates about what God had done for me and what He could do for them. I was told for over ten years that I was disqualified because of my past. One of the men that had led the jail ministry had left the church we had attended together. He contacted me and invited me to go with him to the jail. I began to lead 10 to 20 men each week for five years. One young man had murdered one of our church members. He was drunk and beat an elderly person to death. He attended our meeting one night, and I had the privilege of leading him to Christ. I developed a relationship with him, and right before he was transferred to prison, he smiled at me and said, "I'm so glad I met you. I'm so glad I know Jesus." He is currently serving life in prison.

One of my favorite things to do is walk into that jail. But now I get to share the Gospel of Jesus Christ with rapists, gang members, drug dealers, and every other kind of person you can imagine. I said that I would never return to jail, now I freely go, and it is my privilege. In 2019, God spoke to me, opening my eyes to see that the people were His treasure: the people in prison, in recovery, on the streets. They are the treasure in this lifetime. Having access to the lost is the greatest gift a disciple will ever have this side of Heaven. There is no more incredible feeling than when I see someone I spoke to in jail or recovery serving in my local church with a grateful heart. I thank God each time I witness them getting married or starting jobs they never imagined they would ever get because of their past. I smile as they live a new life filled with freedom in Christ.

Thirteen

Who would have guessed that my life would have been so drastically changed? Certainly not me, but God did. I went from a homeless addict hiding in the woods to becoming a Vice President of the most powerful substance use disorder provider on the planet. I've never felt worthy, not one time when God began opening doors.

Along the way, God began to place specific people in my life intentionally. In the beginning, when I would witness a leader with immense impact, I would attempt to act, dress, and perform like them. Over the years, I discovered I couldn't do their calling, and they couldn't do mine. No matter how hard we try, how many resources we have, or how smart we think we are, the calling on our life comes from God alone.

Authority should never lead to pride, power, and control. It should always lead to a deeper state of humility, responsibility, and most importantly, a deeper state of love and gratitude. Leadership is a privilege. Learning to lead like Jesus is more than an announcement; it is a commitment to lead differently. It is a call to do more, not less.

Once we've tasted God's blessings and grace, we will never want to return to the darkness. That grace and love will flow into the lives of others freely as they poured into our lives. Tasting God's grace forever changes the way we view and respond to others' imperfections and trespasses.

In the year 2000, when I was in prison in St. Joseph, Missouri, I was accepted into a 180-day Cognitive Behavioral Treatment Program called Bridges and Turning Point. After two months, I was given the role of the leader of an essential morning group. This group was designed to encourage the new inmates not to give up on completing the program. If the inmates were to quit the program, they would have to complete their full sentence given by the judge. For many, this meant serving five, ten, or more years of hard time in prison.

Twenty years later, God placed me in the position of leading a nationally known program called, you guessed it, Turning Point. I am in awe of how intentional God is with His plan for our lives. I know that God allowed me to taste a leadership role, then give me a hunger to lead.

When I was in prison, a man would come inside and lead the Sunday church services. I remember looking at him, staring intently, and thinking, "Why? Why would he check into prison and spend his time on someone like me?" I admired him and wondered if I could change my life and do what he was doing for people like me. Later, God would bless me by allowing me to go inside the DeSoto County jails and do just what he did. I had to wait for ten years to be approved, but I have been able to minister to inmates for over six years. I've led thousands to Christ, and many times, been able to walk alongside them after they were released. Most recently, we launched the Celebrate Recovery Inside program for inmates. The men love the program, and I can go inside the pod where they live. It is fun to see them as I arrive. They are sitting at a stainless-steel table, answering questions in their workbooks and studying. I remind them they are being sanctified for God's use, and they are in God's college as He prepares them for battle. They often tell me that they tell their loved ones that they are currently "in college."

I have studied an overwhelming number of leaders from all areas and all types of leadership. I've also served under and personally witnessed all kinds of leaders as well. Sometimes leadership will break your heart. It's so true. I think God shows us these things to let us know that our purpose isn't to put a man on a pedestal but to recognize that God is always the ultimate authority. When I first got out of prison, I had no job. I knew that to stay out of prison, I needed a job fast. I was hired as a temporary worker at the electronics company with the assurance that it would turn into a full-time permanent position soon. Imagine my discouragement when the group that had been hired with me and I were given pink slips. I learned that it was nothing that I had done, but this was their usual way of doing business to keep from paying out benefits to employees. I was very disillusioned, but I later found out that multiple lawsuits had been levied against them because of this practice, and many of them were lost, costing them millions of dollars. I learned a valuable leadership lesson that if you treat your team members wrong and do it so that they cannot fight back, God always brings His justice in the end.

When I led in the church, I discovered many things that I wasn't prepared for that brought division and caused me to question the leaders in the church. Things began to not line up with God's Word. I learned several valuable lessons in witnessing this. When the chain of command is broken, there is always a hidden agenda. In my life, I firmly believe that the enemy sent some of his most skilled soldiers. They were disguised as leaders to destroy me and force me to abandon my mission. It's only been through the power of God's Spirit in me that I was able to withstand the attacks. It has been a harrowing spiritual, emotional, and mental experience that has caused much heartache and pain. I came up with a quote that I often use: "What kind of army destroys its own soldiers?"

I can't think of anything more damaging to God's kingdom than a religious Christian walking around disqualifying those who believe someone else's sin is worse than their own. If you just follow them around for a short period, you will discover they divert attention by judging to hide their own mess. They use religious rules to make them feel superior when it's all a cover-up. They are indeed the ones that should be disqualified. They need to reread the Book—That's why so many churches fail, and it's God that shuts them down.

I discovered deep inside that accomplishing the mission God has given us is more important than having control. Having my feelings hurt, being humiliated, and all of the pain of betrayal is nowhere near as important as staying the course to finish God's race. There is no more incredible feeling in life than to know that you stood on God's Word, didn't take revenge, demonstrated the faith, and won the battle. Never let anyone trick you out of God's calling on your life. Suppose they can manage to get into your feelings and emotions. In that case, you will be tricked into responding in a way that will cause you to be disqualified, disrespected, or fired from your position. Their attacks may be planned, precise, and intentional, but how we choose to respond is everything.

We should strive never to blame God when people hurt us. He often uses injustice to move us to the next assignment He has planned for us. Always seek to look past the pain and into the divine plan. Many people along the way have tried to slow me down in every single role I've had. In the beginning, I almost bought into the tactics, but I've learned they practically always had hidden agendas. Since the time that group of men disqualified me, God supernaturally intervened in so many ways. When I decided to walk away, blessings began to pour out.

Never take any job for granted, no matter how menial that you think it seems. This is a crucial part of being a leader. After I was terminated at my first job in Memphis, I was hired at a logistics warehouse. I was making more money there, but I almost quit the first day because I was discouraged. All I did was ride on a lift and move boxes around from one place to the next. I tearfully asked, "God, don't you have anything more for me than moving boxes from one area to the next? Why do you have me here?" His reply to me was, "I'm teaching you about people." It was at this warehouse that I learned how to share my faith for the first time.

I'll never forget the days I would be riding in my truck with the stereo cranked up real loud. There was a song by Eminem that talks about being willing to take that shot or chance. Would you be willing to do it or let it slip by you? It was those words that helped me decide to take the shot. If God opens the door, take the shot. You can learn later. He equips you along the way.

It was rather scary, honestly, but it was something God commands us to do as believers. I thought about people shouting to others on a street corner and how that was not how I wanted to have to share. Then God brought to mind the people I encounter daily: the over-the-road truck drivers, the men who work beside me in the warehouse. I thought it would be a perfect place to share my faith. Then I thought that maybe my employer wouldn't like it, but I decided to take the shot and do it anyway. I had not planned the conversation when I talked to the man working with me. He was a tough-looking man like he could have been in a prison gang. He was very intimidating, but I simply asked, "Do you go to church?" He looked at me, smiled, and said, "I sure do! I'm the pastor at my church!" From that moment on, I asked that question to everyone I encountered, not only at work but everywhere else as well. I learned that when you are getting your haircut, you have a captive audience.

My newly found treasure of sharing my faith led to our local Celebrate Recovery group growing exponentially. We had 120 attendees per week and many others being led to the church. With that simple question of "do you go to church?" God opens the door to them, at least thinking about God, church, and their relationship with Him. I often saw visible proof when I would see them look up to the sky or down to the ground as I left them. I knew they were thinking about God, and He was doing the convicting in His gentle way. Regardless, I was doing what I was commanded. When you share your faith and see hope come alive as you look into the eyes of people, you will never be the same.

As I mentioned before, Celebrate Recovery was instrumental in creating a hunger for a leadership role. My first night as an Open Share group leader was challenging. We met in an old building in a tiny room. The carpet was stained, and the chairs were old and worn. There were three other men in attendance: one was drunk, one was asleep, and one smelled horrible. I was so nervous as I felt unqualified to lead anything, especially a Christ-centered group. I was trembling and sweating as I recited our small group guidelines. I kept thinking how the God of all creation could reach down and appoint someone like me to lead. I wasn't perfect, I'd never been to college, and I was broken and messed up. Overwhelming fear and discouragement washed over me, but God began to calm my fears. He reassured me that it was by His Holy Spirit and not anything I could ever do that would assure my success.

I would go on to become a Step Study group leader then later a Ministry Leader. Now I am the Celebrate Recovery State Representative for Northwest Mississippi. This role has me responsible for supporting existing and new Celebrate Recovery Ministries in 18 counties in my area of responsibility.

God has used Celebrate Recovery to equip me and teach me valuable leadership lessons. I have learned that anything in life that is not forward-thinking and solution-based is an intense waste of time and resources. I've learned that one should never judge or analyze a human life without a personal invitation. I've also discovered that once a human being has tasted God's grace, it will forever change the way you react and respond to others' imperfections and shortcomings. I'm learning that we all must strive to be an unshakeable vessel of grace to be a real and effective vessel of God's love on this earth.

Over the years, God's Spirit inside me has burned hotter and hotter, and I understand now how to allow His Spirit to lead me and my life. My heart, mind, and spirit always return to the Bible's principles and the leadership lessons of Jesus. I believe the art of allowing the Holy Spirit to lead us is a skill learned through tested faith and God's proven faithfulness. A person can learn to act on the promptings of God as we yield to His control of our steps as Christ-followers and leaders.

Being involved in a small group is so rich. When Jesus went up to pray in the garden before His crucifixion, He had his disciples with him. That was the original small group. Small groups or life groups are one of the most healing and healthy groups on the planet. Meeting regularly with others for fellowship and to study God's Word is a must for a healthy spiritual life. When I began leading my first small group, I had 50 people in our home. It was beautifully crazy. These people would come to the altar following the Sunday morning service, and my wife and I would invite them to our home that very night. We fed them, loved them, ministered to them, and literally became their family. We led many people to Christ in our home, some of whom had been planning suicide that very day. The reward for me is seeing them live each day now with hope and assurance because we were obedient to reach out to them with the love of Christ.

For every door God has opened for me, He's has asked me, "How bad do you want it?" When you want it bad enough, you do everything you can to get it and keep it. I haven't called in sick to work since being released from prison. I've gone to work with my feet bleeding, massive muscle cramps, and intense emotional struggles. I haven't missed or been late on paying a bill for 20 years. How bad do you want it?

I know from experience the importance of reaching youth before they begin to develop bad habits. We have more latch-key kids now than ever before. When I envisioned The Hope Center, I knew that the focus had to be to reach youth. We would do this through activities and common ground scenarios, whether through sports or music or just providing a listening ear. The Hope Center has taught me many crucial leadership lessons, business lessons on being responsible and accountable. I learned to lead and manage a non-profit organization and report to the state to keep our organization running and in compliance. It has taught me to dream big and be bold. It has taught me that surrounding myself with people who have the same vision is an integral part of growing and leading. This is called being equally yoked. Suppose two oxen are not yoked together properly (unequally yoked). In that case, they will not be able to move forward together and will struggle. I am grateful that God has yoked me with those who share my vision and faith at The Hope Center.

In 2020, the Addiction Campuses and Turning Point became Vertava Health. Vertava means "turn + life." Our organization is being transformed into the leader in substance abuse use disorder treatment centers in the world. The executive leadership team is the best of the best. In April 2020, I was promoted to Area Vice President of Operations for Vertava Health. We are a dual diagnosis SUD provider. We offer six levels of care: detox, residential, partial hospitalization, intensive outpatient, and virtual care. At our location in Southaven, Mississippi, we've helped over 5,000 people find freedom from addiction and mental health issues. Our site is a three-story former Holiday Inn hotel. It has a current capacity of 188 patients, and we can care for that many per day.

I love what I do and love the passionate people with whom I get to work. I love the patients. Every day, I thank God that I get to do what I love by helping them and equipping them for success. I share my story almost daily. I am honored to lead a team of over 120 of the most passionate souls on the planet. We have doctors, nurses, therapists, counselors, recovery coaches, housekeeping, dining services, facilities, transportation, psychiatrists, nutritionists, fitness instructors, yoga, art, music, and more. Our vital spiritual component consists of elective groups like NA, AA, Celebrate

Recovery, Church, and SMART Recovery. Vertava Health is expanding with the goal of over 400 locations worldwide. We can do what churches are unable to do. That is, fly people in from all over the United States and help restore hope and freedom to families and give them back their loved ones whole. We receive calls from around the globe at all hours from people seeking help. We are expanding into Memphis in 2021 with a new outpatient program. This organization will soon be known as the leader in our industry.

Another song by Kid Rock talks about being a CEO, or head person in charge, or a role model. When I listened to that song, I thought deep in my heart that I COULD be a CEO one day and a role model for those trying to rebuild their lives after addiction. Being at the bottom instilled in me intense gratitude for everything I experience. When my wife and I built our first home in 2009, I would pull out of the driveway and look up in the sky every morning. I would thank God for every blade of grass and every speck of dirt in that yard. I was living a life I had only dreamed was possible.

I can't stress enough the importance of being humble enough to be led. Submitting to the authority God has placed in our lives is the key to success. When the student is ready, the teacher will appear. Today, I have an incredible Executive Coach and the very best Executive Leadership Team on the planet.

What is in me now wasn't in me before. It's new, and the Bible explains it perfectly. It's God's Spirit. It wasn't in there when I was sitting on that log, addicted and at rock bottom wanting to die. It's new. It's described in detail in God's Word. It's the original and authentic fire of the Holy Spirit of the Living God.

I've experienced both the before and after Christ. I've transformed and lived the reality of His promises. When we belong to God, His promises belong to us. Once one has fully tasted His goodness and accepted this reality, sharing the treasure is not optional. It flows freely through us and into the lives of those that God sends across our path. Many years ago, when I first discovered Facebook, I posted about how thankful I was for what God was doing in my life. A few weeks later, I received a private message from an old friend in Joplin, Missouri thanking me for my post. He stated that because of my posts, he was back in church and doing well. That message lit me up and was the beginning of what I do today.

Recently, I connected with my friend that I ran with through the woods that night from the police. I learned that he, too, had accepted Christ and has been filled with His Spirit. We met together in Springfield and reflected on that long night when God was chasing us. Our smiles were radiant, and the joy of the Lord was overflowing. God is using him and his wife in a significant way in their community and across the globe via social media platforms.

I've had many people attempt to discourage me from doing what I do, but I refuse to silence God's miracles. If someone is trying to prevent you from speaking your heart about God, likely, they don't want anyone else having the mic. Never let any human being trick you out of God's calling on your life.

Another hard truth is sometimes sharing your ideas and dreams with others may not be a good idea. Choose your circle wisely. If you do not, others may take your vision and try to claim it as their own. The pride within a human heart always wants to take instead of joining. There were people that I met that had the resources to help me in my journey. They knew that the ideas were world-class, but they didn't think I was smart enough to bring them to fruition. What their pride didn't reveal to them is that God cannot be outsmarted. When God gives you a dream, no other man, regardless of how rich, smart, or prideful they are, can steal what God has planned for you since the beginning. They think they are powerful, but they will never overpower God.

When I was young, I was consumed with other's opinions and impressions of me. Now, my sole focus is submitting to God through obedience and accomplishing the many assignments He's given me. I learned many leadership traits through learning about them the hard way. One thing I know is that a degree from the Master is the highest form of education. It doesn't come from a certificate, but rather it is embedded deep within the heart. A degree from the Master is much more powerful and effective than a man-given degree. When God develops a human heart and mind for a specific calling, the life experiences educate in ways that man, books, and classrooms cannot.

If you notice, my story and my social media posts point to God and give Him glory because I'm thankful that He decided to save me. He alone transformed my life from the inside out. When I post or write about a victory, the message is always "Look at what God is doing in the life of someone that was lost and addicted with no hope and no reason to go on." My message is that if He helped me, He would help you.

Many people have said for years that they could feel God's presence when I enter a room. They say they can feel it when they join the many programs that I lead. His presence within me is powerful and overwhelming at times. It barely sleeps many nights. I'm so glad that God is using me for His glory and not my own.

Imagine a young man wandering the streets, alleyways, and woods with no hope left. In his mind, his life is over. He's let down his family, loved ones, himself, and God. He's not even sure why he's alive.

Imagine him sitting by himself on a log in the woods all alone, weeping and pleading to a God he wasn't even sure that existed to save him. And then it even gets worse (or so it appears) when God shows up and begins the sanctification process. It's an experience he never would've chosen. Then fast forward two decades, and every single thing in his life is being used to help others discover God and who they are in Him. Our God is so intentional and extremely precise.

God's promises in His Word are for this life and not just eternity. When we do what God instructs, the promises belong to us. I should have died so many times. I now realize when I thought it was over, God had another plan.

Before Christ, I was a liar, junkie, and a thief – lost.

When I arrived in Memphis on that bus with nothing but a backpack, there's one significant thing to note. In that backpack were two changes of clothes I had picked up in the Salvation Army parking lot, two small pendants I had found in the alleyways, and one softcover Bible. You see, it's not the fact that all you have in the entire world is a backpack; it's what's in your backpack that matters.

I had accepted Christ, was being sanctified and was free from man-made chemicals. His spirit was no longer contaminated with man-made substances. I had finally surrendered and won. It was a long and hard road of recovery and transformation, but I allowed God's spirit to lead me. He has sent the best leaders He ever created into my life to equip me for His calling on my life. Great leaders provide for the best destinations.

There aren't words to express the overwhelming peace and freedom I experience every single day of my life. It is truly an incredible feeling to know that I have mastered the art of communication with the broken and hurting. I could only have done that through living my early life as one who was broken and hurting. The gratitude within the depths of my soul belongs to God alone for reaching down and pulling me out of the pit and placing me in the palace - not an earthly palace, but an eternal palace in God's Kingdom.

After Christ, I am a Christ-follower, Master Disciple,

Husband, Father, Friend, Sponsor, Accountability Partner, Master Interventionist, Encourager, Celebrate Recovery State Representative, Church Ministry Leader, Jail Ministry Leader, Area Vice President of Operations, Author, Public Speaker, Archeological Site Founder, Treasure Seeker, and Treasure Finder.

Angels

God's Spirit is on me; He's chosen me to preach the Message of good news to the poor, sent me to announce pardon to prisoners and recovery of sight to the blind, to set the burdened and battered free, to announce, "This is God's year to act!" Luke 4:18-21 MSG

I believe God intentionally and specifically sends His earthly angels into our lives at the precise times to accomplish His will. I always make sure they know I recognize them. The people listed below are indeed God's angels that He used to get me where I am today and lead me. They are priceless and directly from Heaven above. Thank you for listening to God and following your heart. Thank you for believing in me, investing in me, and helping me follow the call God has placed on my life.

Stephanie Dodd , John Wagner, Kenneth McKinney, Matt Morgan, Nadian Zak, Esra Ahmed, Debbie Simmons, Patricia Scott, Denny Burt, Dr. Bartholomew Orr, Reggie Davis, Bobby Scott, Ted Bender, Varina Hopper, Carrie Cahill, Gerald Lang, Laura Taylor, Carmen Kyle, Debbie King, Lee Perkins Caldwell, Phyllis Bailey, and Tricia Toomey

<u>Wise Teachers</u>

TD Jakes, Joel Osteen, Tony Evans, Louie Giglio, Rick Warren, AW Tozer, John Hagee, Dr. John Townsend, and Dr. Henry Cloud

Resources

I believe that many people in recovery have a great treasure and gift they are unaware of at the time. It's a gift that you can't earn, learn, giveaway, teach, or buy. It is a gift that God delivers directly into the heart of those who love him. It's a gift that we acquire through intense pain. This gift is called rock-bottom. I believe it's the greatest gift any human being can receive next to their salvation. My rock-bottom came from being alone in a cell. My rock-bottom came in the form of being utterly alone on the planet. My rock-bottom came in the form of having no visitors for 14 months. My rock-bottom came when no one wanted to hear the phone ring or be in communication with me. My rock-bottom came when I wanted to die, and no one loved me enough to come to see me.

Over a decade after this experience, God revealed the most incredible thing to me. He revealed that is at rock-bottom in which He alone instills unconditional love deep within His children's heart and soul. Once you have indeed been to rock-bottom, you will be able to love others in ways no one else can. I know people who have their Master's degrees, $400,000 homes, and lives that people could only dream of. But they don't have this gift.

I get calls multiple times each week from people asking me to help their children. Why would you call the liar, junkie, and thief in to help your kids? I mean, you have your Master's degree, sometimes seminary degree, and are extremely intelligent and wealthy. Why would you call me? I use this illustration when teaching those in addiction about their gifts. You see, the reason they call me because I've been there because when I tell their kids where I've been, they will listen to me. When I conduct interventions, the first thing I do is tell them I was a liar, junkie, and a thief. Most times, they tell me they're thankful for the talk, and we separate ways. I know at that time, the seed has been planted. I know that God is working now. And I know within a few short weeks He will intervene, and they will be ready to seek out. I learned it is my job to steer them to the resources that are already in place. The number one resource is God alone.

Addiction is the only battle in which total surrender equals total victory. We will not win. God will not stop seeking us. We will tap out. I've discovered that if anyone is struggling, they need to do four things:

1. Go to church at least once a week.
2. Join a Life Group/Small Group.
3. Attend a local Celebrate Recovery Group.
4. Start and complete a Celebrate Recovery Step Study Group.

I've seen it work over a hundred times. Suppose a person is just willing to show up for these four weekly gatherings. In that case, their life will be miraculously transformed by the power of the Gospel being lived out in person and in real life. They will experience the love of God flowing through them through others that have surrendered to Him and are being obedient to the His call on their lives.

Confess your sins to God to be forgiven. Confess your sins to another person to be healed. Through practicing and witnessing this principle in action, I learned that you don't need a "super Christian" (lol) or a super-spiritual person to confess your sins. The healing comes in sharing and total transparency. If you aren't sharing, you aren't healing. This is why the Celebrate Recovery Open Share groups are so important. We have topic-specific groups for all struggles, and even one for Veterans called Welcome Home. These open share groups provide a safe place of belonging and a place to share openly.

Look for a Celebrate Recovery in your town. Go online to www.celebraterecovery.com to find one near you. There are also resources available on the website that will be of tremendous help to you.

Vertava Health offers comprehensive care for addiction recovery and mental health. Vertava Health, formerly Addiction Campuses, is a fully credentialed behavioral healthcare provider of onsite and virtual care services for substance use and co-occurring mental health disorders. Our evidence-based treatment programs designed by licensed professionals help build a comprehensive life in recovery beyond the standard 30-day plan. With residential inpatient and outpatient treatment centers across the country and a national network of healthcare providers, Vertava Health helps individuals get the care they deserve so that they can live out their best future.

We are a compassionate team of licensed physicians, nurses, therapists, case managers, counselors, and recovery coaches who offer individualized treatment plans, comprehensive case management, and a range of didactic, therapeutic, and experiential activities to promote active engagement, practice, commitment, and community.

Our continuum of care spans the entire recovery process from acute detox to residential care to extended outpatient supports, including telehealth. We utilize the American Society of Addiction Medicine (ASAM) criteria and guidance to determine the best placement for each individual, and to offer the most effective care and treatment. Visit www.vertavahealth.com for more information.

I also mentioned The Hope Center Community Center earlier. Being able to give back to the community has been a dream for a long time. I'm so thankful that The Hope Center is an avenue for just that. Through community support and mentor training through the Memphis Grizzlies NBA Mentorship program, our non-profit organization reaches hundreds of youth through activities. It gives them a safe place to go where they can learn about living in today's world.

I'm looking forward to what God is going to continue to do through The Hope Center. I envision more incredible things to come. To find out more, visit www.hopecenter1usa.com.

I can't end without telling more about the Old Route 66 Zoo. What began as just some cool looking rocks has transformed into a micro-art museum from another time. God has used this discovery to reveal Himself to me in the most remarkable ways. I've tried for two decades to prove to myself it wasn't real, but I've given that up. This is the most fantastic art this world has ever seen. It's invisible to the naked eye. You must know the secrets to be able to extract and enhance the scenes. I challenge you to view the pics and the links below. When I discovered this site, I was in bad shape. Since that very day, God stepped in and transformed my life. I'm still in awe as to how He could lead a human being to an exact spot on this giant planet. I'm fully convinced He intends for me to reveal this priceless treasure to mankind. In God's word, it speaks of His handiwork. There's a place on Shoal Creek where the slabs of rocks running out into the creek break and form in animals and man shapes. I can't think of any better example of God speaking through natal creation and nature. That's also the firmament He mentions. I'll go into more detail in a forthcoming book. I hope you enjoy it!

ZOO LINKS

http://portablerockart.blogspot.com/
search?q=Stacy+dodd&m=1
Old Route 66 Zoo Missouri Site 23JP1222

http://www.oldroute66zoo.com/

Facebook - The Zoo

https://www.facebook.com/Old-Route-66-Zoo-Archaeological-Site-346767832000380/

Alan Day - Days Knob

http://www.daysknob.com/SD.htm

About the Author

Stacy Dodd currently lives in Nesbit, Mississippi with his wife, Stephanie. To schedule Mr. Dodd to speak at your organization or church, please contact him at stacydodd67@gmail.com.